MARGARET ATWOOD'S POWER

MIRRORS, REFLECTIONS AND IMAGES IN SELECT FICTION AND POETRY

BY

SHANNON HENGEN

SECOND STORY Press

CANADIAN CATALOGUING IN PUBLICATION DATA

Hengen, Shannon Eileen
Margaret Atwood's power :
mirrors, reflections and images in select fiction and poetry

ISBN 0-929005-49-X

1. Atwood, Margaret, 1939- - Criticism and interpretation.
2. Women in literature.
3. Feminism and literature. I. Title

PS8501.T87Z74 1993   C813'.54   C93-094753-3
PR9199.3.A78Z74 1993

Cover illustration by Laurie Lafrance
Edited by Catherine Marjoribanks

Permission credits appear on page 173

Printed and bound in Canada

*Second Story Press gratefully acknowledges the assistance of
the Ontario Arts Council and the Canada Council*

Published by
SECOND STORY PRESS
*760 Bathurst Street
Toronto, ON
M5S 2R6*

For Agnes Kearns Hengen
(1912-1992)

CONTENTS

❖

ACKNOWLEDGEMENTS

THIS BOOK STARTED in Iowa City, Iowa, in the late 1980s and ended in Sudbury, Ontario, in the early 1990s, so the list of those to thank would be long indeed were every significant name included. Those here comprise a kind of short list.

The book's final version would simply not have appeared had Bruce Krajewski not sustained my commitment to it, through word and deed, even entrusting his laptop computer to me when I needed to travel through northern Ontario in winter. And Gertrud Jaron Lewis, my first Sudbury mentor, deserves thanks for always encouraging my work. The Laurentian University English Department has ever been helpful, including our secretary Helen Curlook; the office of the Dean of Humanities has given appropriate aid, *y compris la secrétaire* Claudette Fasciano; and the Laurentian University Research Fund has contributed generously. Diana Fuller earns much gratitude for all her wonderful distractions.

Iowa City friends and mentors include Mary Lou Emery and Valerie Lagorio; somehow Dee Morris has had a magical, transformative influence on my work, for which I am thankful. Former University of Iowans Bunny Korndorf, Shari Zeck, Dianah Jackson and Sherry Ceniza continue to provide good cheer, and Sarah Witte made life there more human.

Pre-dating even Iowa City are two great teachers Carol Neely and Elin Diamond. I appreciate your getting me started.

Margaret Atwood has been a whimsical, heartening, and co-operative presence. The editors at Second Story Press and Catherine Marjoribanks have offered invaluable advice for revisions, lightening my task.

Karl Skierszkan, who appeared in the comparatively late stages of this project when my energies were failing, and whose cooking revived me, deserves special thanks for many things, not least of which is learning to love the cats. Thanks to them, and of course to the rest of my family, as ever.

INTRODUCTION

"POWER AFTER ALL is not real, not really there," writes Margaret Atwood early in her career, "people give it to each other."[1] Whether idealistic or subversive or both, this statement concerns Atwood throughout her work. Who gives power to whom and why? How do the holders of power wield it? When, why, and how do her characters take power back? How and to whom does it mean differently? Margaret Atwood has published some twenty-four books of poetry, fiction, and criticism, and is a frequent contributor to Canada's major media; in short, "Atwood" is almost a household word in North America, describing a persona many seem to know and think about. Why is Atwood's writing so widely read and taught? What accounts for the central place she holds in the recent development of North American literature?

Beryl Donaldson Langer, in an essay that interweaves the triple threads of Canadian nationalism, North American feminism, and historical materialist theory, writes that Atwood's success derives from her having developed an audience "which is defined as much by class position as by gender or nationality." Specifically, Atwood addresses the "new class," defined as "salaried professionals and technical workers," whose appearance "is one of the distinctive features of advanced capitalism."[2] Donaldson Langer's essay attributes Atwood's success to her reaching that large audience which comprises this new and shifting socio-economic class; I argue further that her writing appeals to these readers because through examination of nuances of moral tone in Atwood's characterizations they better understand their own. For allotments of power remain unequal and its use at times unfair or dangerous even within this apparently homogeneous group.

Canada, for example, is a country often defined as that-which-is-North-American-but-not-American, and female is that-which-is-human-but-not-male; the difference between the terms is power. Atwood's writing in the 1970s, '80s, and '90s has complicated our understanding of relations of power by viewing them from the position of those who have participated least in their entrenchment: Canadian women, for example the mother-daughter pair in *Surfacing*, the persona in *Two-Headed Poems*, and the two Ontario women stranded together on a Caribbean island in *Bodily Harm*. But lest I seem to claim too much "power" for my own readings of Atwood, I quote feminist scientist Donna Haraway, who reminds us of "the structuring of the observer determining the possibility of seeing."[3] In order that my interpretations not seem universalist, I will situate myself (middle-class, white, and female) according to my view of what constitutes the pertinent Canadian historical and literary critical milieux for reading Atwood.

Canada has not historically been interesting to most Americans, nor indeed to many Canadians, who wonder if it exists at all apart from the United States.[4] Such "Americanized" Canadians have often been the men who have worked materially fruitful deals with powerful American men at crucial times throughout Canada's history, arrangements that always bring the two countries' economic bases closer together as they seem to erase other differences between the countries. But in opposition to the Americanized Canadians has stood a group of Canadian nationalists, some in government, some at universities, many writers and artists (including Margaret Atwood), who have argued that Canada's slightly but notably different conception of the economy sets Canada apart from the United States, ensuring other aspects of Canadianness as well. These nationalists espouse not a mindless anti-Americanism but rather an informed understanding of and preference for a Canadian way which, while ideally better than the American way, is also often obscure, unpopular, and impracticable. A Canadian nationalist in these terms is a socialist who opposes US economic and ideological imperialism, and in these terms an American can conceivably have "Canadian" qualities.

Bob White, who writes from this Canadian nationalist perspective, concludes that "much of our uniqueness depends on our social programs and other forms of government intervention that create a more compassionate, caring society than the highly individualistic credo of the US allows."[5] Canada's democratic socialist political tradition has resulted, the nationalists believe, in all that makes Canada worth preserving; for example, "medicare, regional development, crown corporations, environmental safeguards, clean and well-planned cities, cultural institutions such as the CBC, equalization payments," in the listing of journalist David Crane.[6] Strange, naive, or unlikely as such a political philosophy may seem on the North American continent, and though it is currently under severe pressure, it persists in that place which, owing to its physical size as the world's second-largest country and its population, one-tenth of that of the United States, is itself somewhat strange and unlikely. "The shape and nature of the country," writes Canadian journalist Pierre Berton succinctly, "demand that the strong prop up the weak."[7]

Literary critics have almost unanimously found the democratic socialist content of Atwood's writing uninteresting or, when they have sensed it at all, unconvincing;[8] they have by and large ignored it. And she herself has often diverted critical attention from that content in her novels and poetry with an abundance of humour and clever generic or narrative trickery. For Atwood, as she seems to sense, has taken on a double burden in the political thematic of her writing: to articulate not only a kind of Canadian socialism but also its obscurest form, a kind pertaining to women about whose lives and work little has been said. Yet her readers in that "new class" continue to study what integrity is possible for Atwood's women, and men, in changing economic and political times.

The histories of powerful Canadian men are of marginal concern outside the country, and the histories of its powerless women of no concern at all. Yet those characters and their female progeny, not often striking or even especially attractive, have always captured

Atwood's imagination and contribute a feminist perspective on the tradition of Canadian democratic socialism that informs Atwood's politics. Those women represent an ethos which contrasts with that of the men who labour to bring Canada ever closer to union with the United States. Farthest removed from the creation of political ideologies of any kind, the older generation of women in her texts remains tied to home or modest occupations and yet unself-consciously, paradoxically, provides the younger women with a therapeutic legacy. In coming to recognize themselves as Canadian women, the younger figures must newly understand both terms, "Canadian" and "woman," and they interpret "Canadian" to mean what Atwood as nationalist has meant — particularly, those who are left of, or left out of, mainstream America. "Canada has a viable left; the States does not," Atwood claims simply (and Canadian political historians confirm). [9]

The critical problem created by Atwood's project, giving voice and meaning to the twice-obscured histories of Canadian women, [10] affects even the strongest readings of her work. Robert Kroetsch's essay "Unhiding the Hidden: Recent Canadian Fiction" and Margaret Homans's "'Her Very Own Howl': The Ambiguities of Representation in Recent Women's Fiction" occupy prominent places amid the two kinds of criticism containing much of that devoted to Atwood's writing, Canadianist and feminist literary criticism, and both essays interpret Atwood's most often studied novel, *Surfacing*. Both essays, too, for all their strength and deserved prominence, fail to intertwine Canadian socialist politics and Canadian women's histories in reading the novel.

Atwood's language concerns the two critics, Kroetsch perceiving in *Surfacing* a Canadian speech and Homans seeing a language of contemporary women. Kroetsch praises the novel for achieving what he describes as an "uninvent[ion]" necessary for colonized Canadians whose language is the same as its parent countries', a "process of rooting that borrowed word, that totally exact homonym, in authentic

[Canadian] experience."[11] But Kroetsch neglects to indicate that the narrator in the novel finds language only after reuniting with her abandoned parents, more significantly with her mother than her father, just as Kroetsch avoids spelling out what might be the politics of a Canadian language. While Homans emphasizes the narrator's return to her mother, she does not locate the mysterious "maternal silence" in the novel as characteristic of Canadian women's histories, and she does not analyze the ethos which, oddly but certainly, countervails "paternal language" and its American significations.[12]

These two essays witness the importance of Atwood's work to the Canadian nationalist and North American feminist critical movements, movements that share a concern for authenticating languages, as the essays together imply but do not state. At the intersection of those movements in their broader social context, beyond traditional literary criticism, stands Atwood's most powerful work, thus partly explaining her success with a wide readership (not, of course, limited to Canadians or feminists) concerned to study the languages of power as the axes of power shift. The intersection of Canadian socialism in particular and feminism defined as attention to unacknowledged women's pasts describes a thematic site of deep and recurring interest to Atwood;[13] her hope for a socialist-feminist future in North America points, I believe, toward the greatest reaches of her vision.

By introducing the issue of Atwood's power in describing its prime textual location, at the thematic juncture of socialism and feminism, I have arrived at the heart of my analysis. While attesting to her importance, Atwood's critics affirm that she is a powerful writer, yet critics rarely suggest that her power is owing in some way to the stress she gives in her writing precisely to questions of power. Like her modest, almost laborious feminism and her faint and untheorized left-nationalism, Atwood's articulation of power is muted in her novels and poems. Still, her wide international audience, that new class entering or about to enter traditionally empowered institutions, may indeed look repeatedly to her central female figures because they, too, feel both called to change the power relations in their public and private lives and unable to do so.

The issue of power as a phenomenon defined by broader social structures runs throughout all of Atwood's writing, particularly in those works published during and since the Canadian cultural awakening of the 1970s. Of her major texts, I focus on six texts appearing amid and following the Canadian cultural awakening of the 1970s, while also noting her late 1980s' and early 1990s' work in conclusion. "The exercise of power is the opposite of the practice of love,"[14] she writes in an early essay, indicating that power signified negatively to her then, love positively. Yet I believe that in the course of her career she has tried to join the two, seeing the value of the interconnections, redefining and newly politicizing both terms. Power ("American," "male") without love becomes as harmful as love ("Canadian," "female") without power.

In line with the twin social forces of North American feminism and cultural upheaval in the 1960s and 1970s — nationalism in Canada and the antiwar and human rights movements in the United States — Atwood's writing reviews the possibilities of mobilizing power and love by conceiving them anew, defining each from the point of view of its opposite. What, for example, is Canadian power? she begins to ask; what describes a social order in which women govern?

To chart the process of redefinition that her central female characterizations undergo, Atwood's works trace the effects of family and culture upon the formation of identity and therefore lend themselves to interpretation using psychoanalytic theory. My purpose here is to show that her central female characters must attend to their matrilineage and cultural history before they can redefine and change, pointing perhaps to a hope, shared by her readers, for broader social renewal. That such renewal never appears in her writing seems less significant than the hope for it. My approach is primarily psychoanalytic: to develop a language appropriate to describe, in Atwood's writing, the enabling process of identity reformation and, directly connected, the ability to revise language, notably the term "power."

More specifically, some main male characters in her early work are caught in what American psychoanalysis has called "narcissism," a pathological state deriving from cultural disintegration and characterized by feelings of isolation, emptiness, and desperation. Her early women, because they have entered the public sphere and temporarily abandoned their familial and cultural histories, are identified with and defined according to narcissistic men. Then, in the work of the mid- to late 1970s, Atwood begins to critique narcissism as she stresses female characters and their connections not with men but with other women, particularly those in their biological families, in that way developing the pattern of identity formation that might free these women from pathology. Finally, in the texts appearing in the 1980s and 1990s, Atwood interrogates narcissism not only in her male but also in her female characters, women who have gone beyond their mothers by entering the social structures of male power but have not successfully redefined power.

In Chapter One the term "progressive narcissism" will emerge to name a process and its effects differing radically from the psychic state common to Atwood's men in the early and middle work. North American history in the past thirty years will be seen in terms of the advancement of narcissism. A delineation of narcissistic male characters and the kind of power they value comprises Chapter Two, a reading of Atwood's first pair of novels. Chapter Three describes and interprets progressive narcissism as thematic in *Lady Oracle* and *Two-Headed Poems*, texts given primarily to women's interconnections for the first time in Atwood's work. Chapter Four addresses encroaching regressive narcissism in the women appearing in *Bodily Harm* and *The Handmaid's Tale;* Chapter Five in a similar vein reflects upon *Cat's Eye* and *Wilderness Tips*, Atwood's darkest work. A brief conclusion looks as hopefully as possible to the future.[15]

❖

Chapter One

PSYCHOANALYTIC AND HISTORICAL CONTEXTS OF ATWOOD'S WRITING

As an integral figure in the Canadian cultural awakening of the 1960s and 1970s, Atwood hopes to encode in her writing the potentially renewing powers of change. All but one of the central characters and personae appearing in her work from the early 1970s to the early 1980s contemplate becoming specifically Canadian feminists, and their conditions clearly speak to others who question the ruling sociopolitical order in their own environments and would better understand, if not in fact change, that order.

At the heart of inquiry for Atwood's Canadian feminists, from the 1970s to the 1990s, is a revaluation of the term "power": their project is to undermine a sense of power limited to manipulation and domination by a few (the "power politics" of Atwood's earlier work)[1] with a sense of power as distributed among the many and somehow more tolerant, trustworthy, and nourishing. This shift in meaning parallels a redefinition in recent feminist writing in the United States, as, for example, critics Alicia Suskin Ostriker, Carol P. Christ, and Claire Keyes argue.[2] The purpose of this chapter is to develop a psychoanalytic vocabulary to link the Canadian nationalist movement of the 1960s and 1970s with contemporary North American feminism — itself a hybrid — in order better to interpret Atwood's work concerning ideologies of power.

NARCISSISM AND THE MIRROR STAGE

The years 1972-1978 represent a critical stage in Atwood's writing, what I will call a mirror stage, even as they constitute the historical point at which the possibility of a distinctively Canadian conscious-ness came into view. Atwood's novels *Surfacing* (1972) and *Lady Oracle* (1976) and her *Two-Headed Poems* (1978) contain mirror imagery so strategically used that the central speakers' very identities seem coded to it: whereas previously in Atwood's work her central speakers had remained caught in an estranged culture, one dominat-ed by the imperial power ("American" and "male") in relation to which Canadian women formed a kind of white, bourgeois colony, her speakers who newly undergo this mirror stage emerge with iden-tities that struggle to be particularly Canadian and feminist.[3] The process by which they come to call themselves Canadian women,[4] ambiguous as the terms may remain to them, and to speak their own language is a "progressive narcissism."[5]

Psychiatrist Joel Kovel writes that narcissism is a state initiated in early childhood when inadequate parenting, especially the mother's coldness and indifference, prevents the child from developing healthy self-esteem. Seen as a disorder affecting primarily subjects' sense of self-worth, Kovel states, narcissism blocks the two interrelated and central processes necessary for accession to adulthood, the felt need for and ability to identify with others in "a real community ... one grounded in unalienated work and social relations" and the concomi-tant movement "from infantile omnipotence to adult power."[6] Progressive narcissism as I situate it in Atwood's work is, to clarify my term, precisely a state that emphasizes the value of identification with others — nationalistic Canadians and women — and results from a subject's reunion with a mother whose powers the subject had ignored, misunderstood, and rejected. Kovel's conclusion that the mother's personality somehow causes narcissism opposes Atwood's, and indeed that of all other theorists noted here, while his definition of the pathological state remains useful.

Briefly, the mirror stage and progressive narcissism in Atwood's 1970s texts involve a central female speaker's discerning that she cannot recognize, by looking into mirrors, a self she can accept, her deliberately avoiding mirrors until she understands that she must reincorporate a forgotten or lost part of herself, and her finding that part in another woman who is both her biological and ideological mother — always a Canadian. The subversive language her speakers learn at the end of this process has at its heart a sense of power that derives no longer from an imperialistic understanding of the term but from Canadian women's obscure histories. Whereas power means control to the imperialist, it suggests attunement to nature in *Surfacing*, mysticism, endurance, and camaraderie in *Lady Oracle*, and celebration and hope in *Two-Headed Poems*. The final, unrealized goal of the process in the 1980s' and '90s' texts would then be to connect this feminist sense of power with the most promising, existing strain of public power devised by Canadian men, for women and men remain ever mutually dependent in Atwood's work. And Atwood is able to figure such an apparently idealistic image of the mother, beyond her spiteful portraits of individual bad mothers, perhaps because she is the product of a culture with a more or less peaceful and stable history — an adequately parented culture, in other words. This history of good stewardship her personae work to recover as antidote to encroaching imperialism.[7]

In the mirror stage of her writing, Atwood reserves the awakening to progressive narcissism for female speakers and for only certain of them; most obviously, the unnamed narrator of *Surfacing*, Joan of *Lady Oracle*, and the persona in *Two-Headed Poems*. Like narcissistic children, these speakers see only themselves and their immediate contexts, as they must, for the critical moments during which their new identity coheres, thus achieving a more efficacious relationship between self and other. Then in the novel *Bodily Harm*, published in 1983, beyond the mirror stage in Atwood's writing, the central female character is made not just to realize a new self but to imagine its potential efficacy in a global context. But problems arise for this character, as for Atwood's other protagonists of the 1980s and '90s:

these Canadian women come to view themselves as decentred subjects in a world still clinging to the promise of a single, unified North
America restored to full patriarchal authority. And Atwood is of
course not alone in recording increased confusion and ambivalence in
her female characters in the 1970s and 1980s, as Deborah Silverton
Rosenfelt, for example, argues in her piece concerning feminist novels by Toni Morrison, Marge Piercy, Marilynne Robinson, and Alice
Walker, and postfeminist works by Louise Erdrich, Jan Clausen, Sue
Miller, Anne Roiphe, and Atwood.[8]

Mirroring is of course also not unique to Atwood's production.
With reference to the same theoretical vocabulary that I will use to
describe Atwood's speakers' progressive narcissism, Sneja Gunew discusses Australian migrants, for example, who write in English, their
second language, and who are, for a critical moment, like children
who first learn to speak: "in shifting language and culture the
migrant is placed once more in the position of the child. This child is
required to renegotiate an entry into the symbolic — needs to go
once more through a form of the mirror stage, in which a putative
subject is reflected by the gaze of the new host culture, and is quite
other to any previous unified subject." For a "fleeting" moment,
migrant writers must establish their voices as dominant, "reversing
the old oppositions," while ultimately the point is not to establish a
new cultural hegemony but to confront the "unified (or totalising)
orthodoxies" so that "it will be seen as perverse to speak of a unified
Australian culture."[9]

Atwood's central speakers who undergo the mirror stage, like the
Australian migrant writers Gunew describes, learn to speak as
Canadian nationalists only in order to break the imperialist power's
hold on them; progressive narcissism calls them further to imagine,
by redefining power, how hegemony itself might be undermined.
Thus these women come to understand, in a way similar to Eve
Sedgwick in *Nationalisms and Sexualities*, that "this single term
['nation'] is incapable of registering the multiple and incommensu-
rable differences dividing one nation from another (or from itself)."[10]
As sophisticated as their new understanding of power may seem for

its appropriateness to postmodern theories of the decentred subject, this subtle understanding will also be seen to have little real political force in the world of power politics surrounding them. The very Canadian femaleness that they come to accept, however integral to their psychic health, will appear to imply traditional powerlessness owing to the unchanged world into which these female personae reawaken. The powers they inherit remain what Elizabeth Janeway has called "the powers of the weak," political actions or attitudes which "[t]o the powerful ... appear as stumbling blocks, limitations, and misfunctions in the ordained and expected conditions of life."[11]

While "regressive narcissism" as defined by the American male theorist Joel Kovel, noted above, develops precisely as an effect of inadequate mothering in a dominant but troubled culture, Atwood's progressive narcissism locates Canadian women as ego-ideals who remain adequate perhaps because somewhat isolated, in terms of the amount of traditional power they wield, from the dominant culture and its ills. That slight Canadian difference therefore becomes privileged. Beginning with psychiatrist Kovel's definition of regressive narcissism, called simply "narcissism" in American men's theories and in general valorized negatively, I propose to show that Atwood's central women replicate the critique of American men's theories of narcissism advanced by American feminist psychoanalytic theorists, writers whose own sense of mothering is closer to Atwood's in its idealism.

But North American theorists of narcissism rarely undertake a study of literary language, and such a study is crucial to complete the vocabulary necessary for discussion of the mirror stage in Atwood's texts. The phrase "mirror stage" indeed appears in the work of French psychoanalyst Jacques Lacan and provides the terms upon which I base my understanding of the critical period and recurring techniques in Atwood's work.[12] Yet Lacan alone, like the American male theorists, assumes a tone more pessimistic than his feminist commentators (including Atwood); that is, although his linguistic theories provide a necessary link between classical psychoanalytic practice and the study of literary texts, his theories also privilege an inefficacy and hopelessness which his feminist respondents and Atwood circumvent.

The decentred subject mourns the loss of ego integrity and potency in Lacan's scheme, whereas she welcomes their loss in the feminists' view.

Lest the theoretical combination of Lacan and the Americans seem dubious, I refer to the work of US psychiatrist Joseph H. Smith who writes that "Lacan took the American ideal of a strong ego to mean the establishment of a more or less impregnable structure of defense against the truth of human existence. But ... one dimension of ego strength is manifested by the capacity to acknowledge danger, loss, finitude, dividedness, and lack, the capacity to listen to the unconscious."[13] North American critics and theorists can thus override Lacan's distrust of US psychiatry in order to adapt his theories.

Very simply to summarize Atwood's sense of the mirror stage in relation to writing, in her own words, "[l]iterature *can* be a mirror, and people can recognize themselves in it, and this may lead to change."[14] My discussion of current theories of narcissism in the United States, theories which are characteristically culture-bound, will lead to the vital complement of the French school in its attention to language in order to establish terms by which to define the positive transformations Atwood's speakers achieve in their changing world. Just as these 1970s' personae act out the American feminist psychoanalysts' critique of American male theories of narcissism, they follow the patterns traced by the very different French Lacanian feminist theorists.

NARCISSISM DEFINED

Narcissism, as manifested not in the clinical but in the public setting, has been articulated at greatest length by historian Christopher Lasch. Lasch's use of the generic "he" in the following definitive passage from *The Culture of Narcissism: American Life in an Age of Diminishing Expectations* is pertinent and telling in that, throughout this influential text, Lasch studies only powerful American men: "Notwithstanding his occasional delusions of omnipotence," Lasch writes, "the narcissist depends on others to validate his self-esteem. He cannot live without an admiring audience. ... For the narcissist, the world is a mirror."[15] American culture is narcissistic, according to

Lasch, because it has lost both continuity with its past and hope for its future, as the "diminishing expectations" of his subtitle implies. The inadequate parenting that Kovel isolates as a cause of narcissism moves to the cultural level in Lasch's thinking; that is, America can no longer inspire its people with the leadership of a respected parent.

Lasch's description of a narcissist as one who "cannot live without an admiring audience" recalls a group of central male characters in Atwood's novels; David in *Surfacing*, Peter in *The Edible Woman*, Arthur and his radical colleagues in *Lady Oracle*, William in *Life Before Man*, Jake in *Bodily Harm*, and the Commander in *The Handmaid's Tale*. For Atwood's central females, to learn progressive narcissism is to reject the psychic condition of those men.

Narcissistic relations as traditionally defined, Lasch claims, entail a form of interpersonal exchange with exploitation at its centre: narcissists package themselves attractively, then try to get what will further enhance their image from those whom they attract, offering nothing in return because they have nothing but the exchange to offer. When narcissists have gained the desired commodity from the other, they discard the other. Otto F. Kernberg, one of the most prominent American psychoanalysts studying narcissism, writes that "[p]atients with narcissistic personality are extremely self-centred and self-referential, and whatever is going on around them they apply to themselves. ... Narcissistic personalities carry these warped views over into their relationships with other people. They have no empathy for others; other people exist only to serve their needs."[16]

American theories of narcissism such as Lasch's and Kernberg's implicate the surrounding culture. Kathleen Woodward notes that this culture-bound context for psychoanalytic analysis is a distinguishing feature of the American as opposed to the French approach: "the chief contribution of a developmental psychoanalysis such as we find in the work of Erik Erikson or Heinz Kohut is the emphasis on the larger historical context in which the psychological development of the individual takes place, both in terms of social organization and the cultural moment, an emphasis which is almost totally lacking in Lacan."[17]

TOWARD A CULTURAL REVOLUTION

American theorists can view the condition of narcissism as positive or negative depending upon their understanding of feminist optimism for cultural change. A positive value given to the term is often linked to the very processes of identity formation privileging relations with the mother typical of Atwood's women undergoing their mirror stage.

Feminism indeed informs Lasch's more recent text, *The Minimal Self: Psychic Survival in Troubled Times*, in which he clarifies that narcissism —"a disposition to see the world as a mirror, more particularly as a projection of one's own fears and desires"[18] — is indeed a pathological condition. But he describes escape from it in terms indebted to current North American feminist theory, terms connected to Atwood's work in that Lasch, like Atwood's women, has come to privilege the "union" and "dependence" associated not with the public, male sphere but with the private sphere: "The best hope of ordinary unhappiness, as opposed to crippling mental torment — appears to lie in a creative tension between separation and union, individuation and dependence. It lies in a recognition of one's need for and dependence on people who nevertheless remain separate from oneself and refuse to submit to one's whims" (162). In a direct reference to his sources in the work of Stephanie Engel, Nancy Chodorow, Dorothy Dinnerstein, and Jessica Benjamin, Lasch concludes that "the rise of the women's movement appears to strengthen the argument that social change has to go further than a change in institutions or the distribution of political and economic power, that it has to take the form, in other words, of a cultural revolution" (241). However, he argues, "patriarchal values will continue to prevail as long as society assigns children exclusively to the care of women and subordinates the work of nurture to the masculine projects of conquest and domination" (23). Lasch thus argues, and Atwood's women show, that the reintegration and realignment of separated male and female spheres enables that redefinition of power that makes "cultural revolution" possible.

Jessica Benjamin situates Lasch's work with others of its kind and creates a space for her own study:

> In the broadest sense, Lasch and others are engaged in a critique of the effects of rationalization in late capitalism. Rationalization means that impersonal, abstract ways of transmitting values of behaviour, exercising authority, and insuring conformity, have replaced familial communal culture. ... Rationalization means also that authority is no longer located in identifiable personal or symbolic institutions and bonds between people.

Oedipal preoccupations with authority, its decline or imminent return, interest Benjamin less than the possibilities of a cultural critique deriving from the preoedipal experience of "identification with the mother." Those engaged in oedipal critique of hierarchical structures have rightly observed that such authority as there is in contemporary North American cultures resides in "impersonal institutions," and Benjamin suggests that that state is merely a result of a psychology that "stresses separation from rather than recognition of the mother." Although she acknowledges that the family as institution has also been affected by late capitalist rationality and impersonalization, she still implies that institutions can be reformed by subjects whose early learning of differentiation need not reject maternal nurturance; in other words, Benjamin welcomes interdependence just as Lasch and Atwood do. The father's promise of freedom can be better kept along with the mother's promise of nurturance, Benjamin concludes, stating that "[t]rue differentiation means accepting dependency not as dangerous regression but as enjoyable connection."[19]

KINDS OF POWER

Adopting the role of feminist historian, Marilyn French studies how the structures of women's power have been dismantled and devalued across cultures over time. The central argument of her *Beyond Power* is as follows: "To become dominant men had to splinter women's power in three ways: they had to break the bond of mutual affection between men and women and substitute a bond of power; to break the bond of unity among women; and to break the bond of love between women and children, substituting a bond of power between men and children." Like Lasch and Atwood, French argues that "what is necessary is revaluation of the value of power itself ... and revaluation of other, less respected qualities." Those "less respected qualities" French associates with Afro-American and women's cultures: "intermeshed, communal and flexible, black culture is bound by bonds of love and friendship; it is a 'feminine' culture in that sense." Non-material or spiritual values, recalled by the maternal histories in Atwood's work, appear similarly in French's study as the basis for a redefinition of masculine power. "This is the feminist goal," French writes: "to reintegrate humanity requires not just treating women as human beings, but valuing in one's own life and actions love and compassion and sharing and nutritiveness equally with control and structure, possession and status."

Social psychologist Hilary M. Lips corroborates French's views of the effect of patriarchal institutions upon the family but adds that even traditional power within familial relations must continue to be acknowledged, for "in a family, all members relate to one another in terms of power as well as, or instead of, affection." And, "[w]e cannot eliminate power over some people by others, because influence is a necessary part of our web of interactions with others." Our interpretation of "influence" will of course determine our use of power, and our use of power will in turn be decided by the presence or absence of "inner strength," arising from "persons' connecting with one another and with their environment."[20]

French's observation that, even at the fundamental level of language, power in its ordinary usage determines meaning — "syntax in most Western languages is representative of a power relation: a doer does to a done to"[21] — recalls two of her contemporaries, George Steiner and Carol Gilligan. Steiner asserts, rather like the French feminist psychoanalytic critics whose theories I discuss below, that "traditional syntax organizes our perceptions into linear and monistic patterns. Such patterns distort or stifle the play of subconscious energies, the multitudinous life of the interior of the mind."[22]

Concluding her empirical, comparative study of psychological development in women and men, Gilligan remarks: "My research suggests that men and women may speak different languages that they assume are the same, using similar words to encode disparate experiences of self and social relationships. ... At the same time, however, these languages articulate with one another in critical ways." Thinking beyond one of the major insights of contemporary North American psychology, that women are socialized through relationship with others and men through separation, Gilligan suggests that both genders are capable of mature identities which combine traditionally male and female roles, given the complex choices now open, especially to women, as a result of the successes of feminism. She describes as one of "the paradoxical truths of human experience" that "we know ourselves as separate only insofar as we live in connection with others, and that we experience relationship only insofar as we differentiate other from self."[23]

Gilligan writes, in response to a symposium on *In a Different Voice*, that "my critics essentially accept the psychology I call into question — the psychology that has equated male with human in defining human nature and thus has construed evidence of sex differences as a sign of female deficiency." What theorizing from women's experiences might provide is illumination of "the psychology of nonviolent strategies for resolving conflicts."[24] Like Benjamin, Gilligan distinguishes between oedipal and preoedipal models of cultural critique; while Atwood does not use such terms explicitly, she does view dominant ideologies that are male-conceived or given to the language of oedipality as lacking in the particular revolutionary power of feminist or preoedipal critical vocabulary.

KINDS OF LANGUAGE:
THE IMAGINARY AND THE SYMBOLIC

While French feminist psychoanalysts Julia Kristeva and Luce Irigaray proceed not from cultural studies but from intrapsychic theories indebted to Lacan, they arrive at conclusions that are hopeful in the same way as are Benjamin's, Gilligan's, and Atwood's. Both French theorists privilege that state of union with mother which, in North American terminology, is called "preoedipal" and which, in the French psychoanalytic school deriving from Lacanian theory, is called "the Imaginary."

Accession to language marks the child's exit from "the Imaginary" into "the Symbolic," the lifelong condition characterized fundamentally by a desire for reunion with the mother's body. Language can never fulfil that desire, but neither can its use be avoided. The issue for feminist revisionists of Lacanian theory is to describe a language that simulates a return to the Imaginary in its subversion of the intervening Symbolic order. In these theorists' terms, the Imaginary is maternal and the Symbolic paternal; language that does not question the Symbolic paternal order also does not fulfil desire.

According to Lacan, in his essay on the mirror stage, all forms of identification are narcissistic in that they ultimately fail to satisfy the desire for reunion with the mother. Language learning becomes possible, he argues, only after children become capable of symbolization, and children become capable of symbolization only after having recognized themselves as separate from mother. Prior to that initial and alienating moment of self-identification Lacan calls the mirror stage, children do not speak and indeed do not need to speak because their basic demands are otherwise expressed. After the child becomes visually aware of separation from mother and of mother's relationship with father, the child comes to speak. Language intervenes as a system of symbols and must displace the earlier noises by which demand was voiced. Within the symbol system of language, the child learns further separation, division, differentiation and is ever further removed from the Imaginary stage of fusion with mother.

Both male and female children learn differentiation from mother as they learn the many differentiations within language, a central one being that between male and female. If construction of the speaking subject takes place as Lacan proposes, then male subjects will be those whose powers of symbolization most alienate them from the completion of infancy. Males learn the following economy from mother and father: father has mother and in order to get mother, son has to be like father and will therefore identify with him.[25] In this early narcissism the subject takes from mother's and father's language a substitute for libidinal fulfilment and is shaped by that language: relations of power between mother and father structure the child's perceptions as a gendered subject. Father is a man, and men under patriarchy are typically those with economic and political power gained precisely through mastery of symbolization.

Narcissism, as defined by French psychoanalysis indebted to Lacan, is a process beginning in early childhood and involving subjects' libidinal investment in others in an effort to return to the Imaginary. If the subject invests in others who are more successful in the Symbolic than in the Imaginary, then the subject is headed for the acquisition of economic and political power. If subjects oppose the effects of that power they can attempt to return to Imaginary processes, attending to the vulnerable unity of the mother-child dyad in order to redefine and — ideally — mobilize it. Early emotional life and its subversive power indeed supplies the model for revisionist speech in both Kristeva's and Irigaray's theories.

Kristeva's early theory of what she refers to variously as "poetic language," the "poetic work," "poetic logic," and "dream logic"[26] is especially attractive for my interpretive purposes because it argues for the powers of poetic language not only to subvert the oppressive ruling order but also to suggest a method of returning subjects to fusion with mother, processes that become simultaneous. Kristeva believes, along with the Russian Formalists, that "society may be stabilized only if it excludes poetic language" (31), the language spoken by the least powerful. She asks, "if we are not on the side of those whom society wastes in order to reproduce itself, where are we?" (31). Poetic language disrupts literal language as well as formal sound and syntax and is thus associated with pre-linguistic experience. The following passage from Kristeva's *Desire in Language* explains that:

> The semiotic activity, which introduces wandering or fuzziness into language, and a fortiori, into poetic language, is from a synchronic

point of view, a mark of the workings of drives (appropriation/rejection, orality/anality, love/hate, life/death) and, from a diachronic point of view, stems from the archaisms of the semiotic body. Before recognizing itself as identical in a mirror and, consequently, as signifying, this body is dependent vis-à-vis the mother. At the same time instinctual and maternal, semiotic processes prepare the future speaker for entrance into meaning and signification (the symbolic). But the symbolic (i.e. language as nomination, sign, and syntax) constitutes itself only by breaking with this anteriority, which is retrieved as 'signifier,' 'primary process,' displacement and condensation, metaphor and metonymy, rhetorical figures. ... Language as symbolic function constitutes itself at the cost of repressing instinctual drives and continuous relation to the mother. (136)

In her essays, Atwood has echoed Kristevan theory in posing a question strikingly similar to Kristeva's concerning poetic language. Atwood states that in oppressive regimes poets are often among the first to be silenced. As she points out in *Second Words* (1984), "how many poets are there in El Salvador? the answer is none."[27] Atwood and Kristeva thus agree on the potentially subversive power of language, however their views of what constitutes poetic language may differ. Briefly — and I will return to this point in Chapter Three — Atwood tends to believe that a plain style is subversive in a North America in which formal experimentation is fashionable and marketable, whereas the early Kristeva equates subversive writing primarily with formal experimentation. Atwood's writing is not remarkably innovative in form, but her obsessive use of the rhetorical figure of the mirror remains a direct link between Kristeva's theory of an aesthetic of subversion and Atwood's practice.

The potential harmfulness of Kristevan theory and Atwoodian practice have been suggested. Kaja Silverman's critique of Kristevan semiotics, for example, notes that Kristeva's examples of subversive writers are exclusively male; indeed, writes Silverman, "the artist is necessarily male for Kristeva" because the maternal, finally, implies silence. Silverman's provocative and unorthodox reading of Kristevan semiotics urges feminist psychoanalytic criticism to "recognize the unconscious mother for who she is, the Oedipal rather than the pre-Oedipal mother" — a figure equally implicated in the Symbolic as is the father.[28] Marianne Hirsch, like Silverman, interprets return to the mother as regressive, in this case concerning Atwood's novel *Surfacing*: "To posit, even tentatively, a space outside of ideology and patriarchy is to support and participate in that very ideology, rather than to attempt to undermine it" through "mystification of a pre-oedipal realm."[29] While these readings perhaps explain why Atwood's characters have yet to achieve political efficacy, they also seem premature, for the real effects of feminist poetic logic upon a late capitalist habit of mind have never been assessed. To refuse to imagine that antipatriarchal leadership, influenced by some version of Kristevan semiotics, might still emerge in North America seems hasty, for benevolent allies in that hope ought to be encouraged no matter how indirect or impractical their strategies may seem.

In one of Kristeva's more recent books, *Black Sun: Depression and Melancholia*, she writes simply about dream logic: "How can one approach the place I have referred to [the semiotic chora, or 'Thing']? Sublimation is an attempt to do so: through melody, rhythm, semantic polyvalency, the so-called poetic form, which decomposes and recomposes signs." Later she explains that merely the "excess of affect" can "produce new languages — ... poetics." And, as if in tiny summary of her theory of the origins of language — poetic or other — she states: "since I consent to lose her [both the real mother and fantasmic Phallic Mother] I have not lost her (that is the negation), I can recover her in language."[30] Thus Atwood's plain poetic style constitutes a potentially subversive force, implicitly, as does all poetry, but also explicitly in moments when the poetic voice literally recalls the mother's body.

"FEMINIST" NARCISSISM

In her theory of feminist narcissism, Irigaray concerns herself not with forms of poetry but with the structures of Western philosophical and psychoanalytic thought. She comments in an interview concerning her project in *Speculum of the Other Woman* that "women must continue to struggle for equal pay, for social rights, against discrimination, at work, in education, etc. But that is not enough: women who are simply 'equal' to men would be 'like them,' and therefore not women. Once more, the sexual difference would be cancelled, misunderstood and glossed over. One must invent, amongst women, new forms of organization, new forms of struggle, new challenges."[31] And she looks toward the point from which women must start to discover those "new challenges":

> the fact remains: the relationship of women to their mothers and to other women — thus towards themselves — are subject to total narcissistic "black out"; these relationships are completely devalued. Indeed, I have never come across a woman who does not suffer from the problem of not being able to resolve in harmony, in the present system, her relationship with her mother and with other women. Psychoanalysis has totally mythologised and "censored" the positive value of these relationships.[32]

In the title section of *Speculum* Irigaray describes the central problematic of woman's attempt to "resolve in harmony" her female interconnections. The Lacanian mirror stage leaves subjects estranged from themselves and victimized by the estrangement unless they can recognize the inevitability of that and all subsequent narcissistic phases. Irigaray asks how antifeminist narcissism operates:

> Are we to assume that a mirror has always already been inserted, and speculates every perception and conception of the world, with the exception of itself, whose reflection would only be a factor of time? Thus extension would always already be re-staged and re-projected by the subject who, alone, would not be situated there. Does the subject derive his power from the appropriation of this non-place of the mirror? And from speculation? And as speculation constitutes itself as such in this way, it cannot be analyzed.[33]

It is precisely the power of patriarchy to hold the gaze in which woman is seen only as man would see her, in his image, or as a mirror reflection of his gaze, that Irigaray would subvert by proposing a feminist narcissism which would not only shatter patriarchy's "old dream of symmetry"[34] but would further allow for the articulation of differences among women. She suggests, beyond the classical psychoanalytic tenet that all normal women must ultimately accept the secondary roles of wife and mother and accept the roles as secondary, that "the woman and the mothers are not mirrored in the same fashion. A double specularization in and between her/them is already in place. And more. For the sex of woman is not one. And, as jouissance bursts out in each of these/her 'parts,' so all of them can mirror her in dazzling multifaceted difference."[35]

The process I will chart in Atwood's progressive narcissism is like what Irigaray describes as an alternative to the identity formation that perpetuates patriarchal, antifeminist, or regressive narcissism. But the result of the mirror stage, whenever it occurs, is the acquisition of language, and in order to describe the language Atwood's central women learn in their retreat from the ruling Symbolic order, I will draw upon Kristevan semiotics. Linguistic processes recalling the Imaginary in Kristevan theory include "displacement and condensation, metaphor and metonymy, rhetorical figures," relocating Freud's description of the dream work ("displacement and condensation") into waking speech. Kristeva further associates "metaphor and metonymy" and "rhetorical figures" with poetic and dream logic and thus with speech closer to the Imaginary.

The rhetorical figure that creates the central problematic for Atwood's development of a progressive narcissism is the mirror, as I will show at some length in the chapters that treat her texts. For Atwood's women undergoing the mirror stage, as for Irigaray and for Anglo-American feminist literary critics, the mirror is a figure so laden with significations of antifeminist narcissism that women cannot see past it to one another and to social change. Atwood's central women argue fervently that the figure of the mirror serves neither the men who invoke nor the women who face it.

In summary, the psychoanalytic theorists cited here concur that narcissism implies unregulated self-esteem, that which represents subjects as uncomfortably inadequate. This faulty self-esteem originates from failed mirroring in one of three moments: before oedipality (in Kohut's and Kovel's theories),[36] at the moment of accession to language (in Lacan), or during the process of oedipalization when authority becomes internalized to form the superego (in Kernberg and Lasch). Kohut, in not addressing oedipalization and therefore not addressing subjects' relations to authority, can advocate a therapeutic narcissism in which the analyst, an authority, simply stands in for the parent who withheld approbation, giving the patient an adequate sense of self. Lacan eschews the concept of an adequate sense of self or healthy self-esteem, linking psychic maturity instead with a resignation to narcissism as an ever-desiring, ever sadly unfulfilled ego state, while Smith argues for a reinterpretation of Lacan's concept of the ego. Kohut, Kovel, and Lacan similarly dismiss broader cultural issues, while Lasch and Kernberg do not. Narcissism is neither therapeutic nor tolerable to the latter two, but rather a disorder imposed by a culture in decline.

Feminist theorists Woodward and Benjamin imply within their critiques of narcissism as a male-defined disorder a reappropriation based upon early childhood experience. Their work, initially like Kohut's in privileging the preoedipal mother-child dyad that precedes acknowledgement of the father, would mobilize the powers of that dyad to critique the intervention of language and its attendant authoritarian systems. What matriarchal or preoedipal language might be or express becomes the basis of Kristeva's theory, and the ways in which women might propagate a more radically feminist narcissism by displacing phallic power concerns Irigaray.

Kristeva's concept of poetic language suits my treatment of Atwood's poetry, particularly *Two-Headed Poems*, while an Irigarayan idea of mirroring underlies my study of Atwood's fiction, the place where Atwood's understanding of the process of progressive narcissism gradually emerges. For clarity, I will distinguish once again between Atwood's sense of the mirroring effects of literature, among its central functions in her view, and the figure of the mirror itself. The texts can provide the kind of mirroring she values, that which calls for change, a mirroring like the process of progressive narcissism as undergone by certain of her female protagonists, whereas the specular figure in her texts always threatens to signify regressive narcissism.

Irigaray's call for feminist narcissism most nearly suits the mirror stage and its results occurring in Atwood's work after 1972. Irigaray, however, makes no reference to particular cultures, and in order to show how both regressive and progressive narcissism begin to unfold in the Canada of the past twenty-five years, I will now turn to a brief chronology.

HISTORICAL CONTEXTS

Canadians have perceived themselves as tied somehow to Americans increasingly since the decline of British power following the Second World War, and Canada's own ever-changing conditions have mixed with continual alterations in the American situation to produce a state of constant and, in Atwood's view, dangerous instability. Psychoanalytically, this condition produces narcissistic subjects because of the absence of parent or parent symbols whose mature attitudes to authority their children inherit. Historians Robert Bothwell, Ian Drummond, and John English record that within its boundaries anglophone Canada saw the optimism of 1960s' economic prosperity, political stability, and social renewal undermined by the crisis of 1970s' Quebec separatist activities and instabilities in the world market; looking south, in turn, Canadian opinion altered from fascination with the Kennedys and their administration to disillusionment at the assassination, race riots, and the war in Vietnam.[37]

To summarize Canadian-American relations during the late 1960s and early 1970s when Atwood's *The Edible Woman* and *Surfacing* were published (the objects of study in Chapter Two), I quote Bothwell et al., who write that, in Canada, "[t]his new self-confidence, this sense that Canada was a better nation and Canadians a better people, struck us suddenly" (279), "better" presumably than its parent countries. With Canada's own serious political and economic problems in the 1970s came a chastening of nationalism, however; at the same time, the historians observe, "[i]n 1960, *Maclean's* had called America the land people are shouting about; by 1967 it was the land people were shouting at" (341). But as the historians note and current trends in Canadian politics attest,[38] Canadian left-nationalists have continued throughout this turmoil to study the possibilities of maintaining an identity which, in its different material base, is not entirely imported from the United States, an identity Atwood begins to consider in her second novel, *Surfacing*.

The Canadian government has typically, throughout its history, worked toward a "joining together of the radical and liberal traditions" (260) in a mode both like and unlike the dominant ideologies of English Canada's models, the United States and Britain. While the Canadian government has defined itself primarily in relation to the United States for the past twenty-five years, to conclude, it is at its most radical when least closely allied with the American economy — when defined in opposition to the United States — and at its least radical when most defined in American terms. Atwood's concern to provide her characters with Canadian speech allies her with an ongoing tension in Canadian political culture at large.

The left-nationalist political tradition in Canada, with which Atwood will ally her female speaker in *Two-Headed Poems*, begins to undergo a serious threat in the Canada in which that text and *Lady Oracle* (the subjects of Chapter Three) are published. Historians Bothwell et al. write:

> By 1977 the polls were showing that the majority of Canadians had "very great" or considerable confidence in American foreign policy. [Then-Prime Minister] Pierre Trudeau courted the American capital's favour. The debate about Canada's future was carried on most eloquently in the depths of Wall Street and the halls of Congress. Trudeau ... developed a good relationship with ...

Gerald Ford ... [and] Jimmy Carter. In contrast to the Vietnam years, when close ties with an American president would have given rise to charges of sell-out or "complicity," Trudeau's warm reception in Washington and his equally warm response garnered press and public approval in Canada.[39]

Through the character of Nate in her 1979 novel *Life Before Man*, Atwood will critique Trudeau's handling of The October Crisis (1970) when his government invoked the War Measures Act, "declaring that an 'apprehended insurrection' existed in Quebec and giving the police extraordinary powers of arrest and detention against anyone suspected of belonging to, or sympathizing with, the F[ront de] L[ibération de] Q[uébec]";[40] through her English-Canadian speaker in the 1978 volume of poems she attacks the Prime Minister's increasing friendliness toward Washington, an attitude the speaker sees as economically valuable but ideologically fatal. Trudeau asks Canadians to accept American imperialism for economic reasons while he avoids what Atwood's speaker argues will be the inevitably attendant erasure of Canadianness.

THE FREE TRADE AGREEMENT

Serious enough economic problems emerged following the Trudeau years to bring Canadian and American leaders to enact a broad, controversial trade agreement designed, from the Americans' perspective, chiefly to open Canada's impressive natural resources (those celebrated most obviously in *Two-Headed Poems* but throughout Atwood's work) to the American consumer. What might remain of Canadian socialism when Canadian resources and the products of Canadian labour receive no tariff protection understandably concerned not only Atwood, ever the left-nationalist, but also many others. "[S]uspicion among Canadians over a free trade treaty with the United States has been growing on both economic and cultural grounds," reports Mark Nichols in the 4 January 1988 issue of *Maclean's*. The report, assessing a poll of 1,500 Canadians in fall 1987, continues: "The findings also indicated that a substantial majority — 79 percent of those polled — were conscious of being different from Americans and proud of many of the beliefs and institutions that contribute to their national identity. As well, 49 percent were concerned that free trade would make it harder for Canadians to maintain the things that they believe make Canada unique."[41] The "things" Atwood believes "make Canada unique" appear in some detail in the novel *Bodily Harm* (the subject, with *The Handmaid's Tale*, of Chapter Four).

Atwood published her seventh novel, *Cat's Eye*, in 1988, the same year that an election was called by the governing Progressive Conservative party in Canada. Both the novel and the Conservatives succeeded (as will be discussed in the final chapter). The New Democratic Party, the social democrats, fared better than ever in the fall 1988 federal election, gaining 20 percent of the popular vote and 43 seats in Parliament (the Liberals gained 32 percent and 83 seats). However, the Progressive Conservatives, who in this election campaign were fundamentally requesting a mandate for free trade with the United States, achieved not a majority of popular votes (they got only 43 percent) but the more significant plurality of legislative members (168 seats) and won the election.

As a result, the Free Trade Accord was signed on 1 January 1989 by then-Prime Minister Brian Mulroney and then-President Ronald Reagan. *Maclean's* magazine devoted most of its 4 July 1989 issue to a comparative study of the two countries, and its senior contributing editor, Peter C. Newman, attests in his essay "Bold and Cautious" that "[w]hat the Americans have always wanted is to control our resources and the profitable parts of our economy, without the trouble and expense of colonial administration. They are in the process of achieving just that, indirectly, through the recently signed Free Trade Agreement, the last of several attempts on both sides of the border to unite the two economies."[42] Lawrence Martin studies the effects of the agreement and other policies of the Mulroney government in his book *Pledge of Allegiance: The Americanization of Canada in the Mulroney Years*.

> While the recession's effects made it difficult to disentangle the pros and cons of the trade agreement, there was one clear consequence upon which both sides agreed. This was the rapid pace of Canada's integration and harmonization with the United States. Beyond the basic provisions of the historic [free trade] accord, what was tellingly registered was the psychological impact. The free trade agreement triggered a turn in the public mind, a new consciousness among Canadians that they were now members of the American economic system.

Martin continues to pose the question plaguing nationalistic, as opposed to continentalist, Canadians (those who favour integration with the United States): "Would Canada's economic integration with the United States lead to other forms of integration?" His research shows that the majority of Canadians fear the explicit and implicit results of the unprecedented melding of the two countries during free trade. "In a Gallup poll taken in the autumn of 1990," Martin writes, "65 per cent of Canadians said that their lifestyle was influenced too much by the Americans. ... Opinion on the free trade agreement itself had grown increasingly negative, largely because of the recession. By almost a two-to-one margin, the agreement was opposed." Concerning the proposed North American Free Trade Agreement (NAFTA), designed to draw Mexico into an American-style economy, Martin states that a high-ranking Canadian government official expected opposition from the "'old left-wing, crypto-communist, anti-free trade, NDP-Liberal, con group,'" of which Atwood would certainly be considered a member.[43]

In one of her anti-trade-deal pronouncements, Atwood links — as ever — feminist with socialist issues, while critiquing the advertising strategies of the Progressive Conservatives during the election campaign. As usual, she also attacks pro-American Canadian men in observing:

> *Real men don't eat quiche or oppose the deal.* This was not a Tory slogan, but it might as well have been. Great efforts were made to depict any who raised questions about the deal as thumb-sucking,

safety-blanket, sheltered-workshop wimps, sissies deficient in male gonads.

Trouble is, half the voters are women. Women do not scream and faint when told they aren't real men. ... Also, those with legitimate concerns — including pensioners, mothers, and business people and workers in many areas from needle trades to nursing to beer and wine to computer billing — felt they were being insulted and bullied for even raising these questions.

...

Just the Toronto literati oppose the deal. ... But with 50 per cent opposition to the deal and only 30-some for, either it's *not* just the Toronto literati, or this has been the most successful creative writing program in history.[44]

The most "Americanized" men (as I defined the term in my introduction), those who most thoroughly adopt an American capitalist-imperialist ethic, are always the least sympathetic in Atwood's texts (Peter as articling lawyer in *The Edible Woman*, movie-making communications teacher David in *Surfacing*, city planner William in *Life Before Man*, Jake in *Bodily Harm*, Ian in *Wilderness Tips*, for example) because they represent the group of more or less traditionally powerful Canadian men who have always opted to link Canada's mixed economy more firmly with American capitalism. Not themselves politicians, these characters nevertheless promote Americanization through their subtle complicity with it. Less "Americanized," more Canadian men in Atwood's texts (Duncan in the first novel, Joe in the second, Nate in the fourth, Daniel in the fifth, and Eric in the most recent book of short stories, for instance) can in turn be associated with Canadian men who historically have argued to preserve the Canadian difference, men who, like Atwood, though less explicitly, promote left-nationalism.

That Atwood began publishing at the start of Canada's own mirror stage, the maturation of its sense of self as potentially ideologically independent, argues for my sustained attention to issues of identity formation, not just in those Canadian characters headed into what remains of traditional power structures amid changing times, but also in those characters who have never experienced positions of power and accede to them with difficulty. The lack of reference to Canadian women in the above overview, finally, justifies Atwood's subtle feminist project: to show the directions she urges Canadian women to take in their alliances with men and with American feminists to support a distinctively Canadian future.

❖

Chapter Two

MIRRORS, MEN, AND EMPOWERMENT: THE FIRST TWO NOVELS

NARCISSISTIC MEN profoundly affect the central female characters in Atwood's first two novels, *The Edible Woman* (1969) and *Surfacing* (1972). Although not all of the men in these texts are regressively narcissistic, in each, at least one significant male figure is; this fact witnesses Atwood's sense of the pervasiveness of regressive narcissism in the cultural situations that the texts mirror and critique. Marian in *The Edible Woman*, a market researcher, and *Surfacing's* narrator, an illustrator, allow their identities to be shaped and their conceptions of personal power to be determined by men who, in varying degrees, cannot come to terms with their own identities and sense of power. The confusion Atwood's men experience in these novels mirrors the dramatic cultural upheaval ongoing in Canada when the texts were produced, upheaval resulting in conditions that can produce narcissistic personalities while also continuing to ensure the disenfranchisement of talented young Canadian women, like those with whom the men interact.

Atwood's central female fictional voices could be said to add both substance and nuance to her radical cultural beliefs.[1] Describing Canada in a 1978 interview as "an alternative North American society,"[2] Atwood continues:

I think the reason for wanting to have a Canada is that you do not agree with some of the political choices that have been made by America, and that you want to do it a different way. One that's fairer to the environment, not as hostile to Nature, has a more egalitarian view of citizenship, a more co-operative view towards how the economy should be run—instead of ruthless individualism, every man for himself, the kind of thing you get in the States. And that has been the Canadian way: we've been forced into having co-operatives, we've been forced into a number of things because we're poorer.

In a 1973 interview, she further affirms her nationalism when she outlines a "third thing" she worked to thematize in *Surfacing*. She states that "[y]ou can define yourself as innocent and get killed, or you can define yourself as a killer and kill others. I think there has to be a third thing again: the ideal would be somebody who would neither be a killer [n]or a victim, who could achieve some kind of harmony with the world, which is a productive or creative harmony, rather than a destructive relationship towards the world." But the "creative harmony" is only as empowering as its cultural milieu will tolerate.

Especially wary of what she calls "the great Canadian victim complex," Atwood continues: "If you define yourself as innocent [as the narrator of *Surfacing* tries to do early in the novel] then nothing is ever your fault. ... And this is not only the Canadian stance towards the world, but the usual female one." More, "if you are defining yourself as innocent, you refuse to accept power. You refuse to admit that you have it, then you refuse to exercise it, because the exercise of power is defined as evil."[3] And Atwood refers to "a third language" she believes her narrator in *Surfacing* needs, explaining that "a very Canadian concern at the moment" is "a concern with language" because "the literary tradition that history provided us with was created in another country,"[4] just as were — historically — Canada's choices of political ideologies.

Atwood's developing nationalism thus seems rather open-ended, providing no explicit set of assumptions to be labelled "Canadian," and her position echoes Kristeva's views of French nationalism *vis-à-vis* acceptance of foreigners. Fearing the closure that a rigid definition of "Frenchness" implies, Kristeva advocates "no longer ... welcoming the foreigner within a system that obliterates him but promoting the togetherness of those foreigners that we all recognize ourselves to be." Nationalism, Kristeva argues, as an effect of "the bourgeois revolution ... has become a symptom — romantic at first, then totalitarian — of the nineteenth and twentieth centuries."[5] Atwood takes pains to define her nationalism as anti-totalitarian, it seems, both in her direct references to the Canadian "third thing" and in the subtle working out of such a position through fictional characterization and poetic voice.

THE FIRST NOVELS

Throughout her sustained search for Canadian language, Atwood's pivotal texts (those I treat second in each of the pairs I study) represent the clearer and stronger statements on pressing issues in their cultural milieux, as though the fictions and characters preceding those pivotal texts also enable them, demand this of them. *The Edible Woman* anticipates *Surfacing* in that its central female character remains confused in her identity and muted in her speech because she is defined in relation to "Americanized" males. What distinguishes *Surfacing* is precisely that its female protagonist, the unnamed narrator, begins to recognize her enclosure in those males' perceptions and to imagine a way out. In so doing, the narrator stands at a pivotal point in Atwood's work as she begins the complex journey back to her mother, "mother" country, and mother tongue.

Narratively, the second novel advances what the first initiates: in both, a woman arrives at a clearer sense of self by interacting with contrasting male figures and by tentatively allying herself with the one who is quieter, more introspective, less dangerously narcissistic than the others. In both, the woman simultaneously realizes the crucial importance to her of other women — a negative and unusable realization for Marian in *The Edible Woman* but a positive and practical one for the central character of *Surfacing*. While Atwood's own vocabulary lacks a term for the process which her first two novels discover (the "third thing" she referred to in her criticism), "progressive narcissism" precisely names the process.[6] Coded to mirror imagery, its effect is to arrive at a Canadianized sense of the term "power."

My interpretation builds upon existing scholarship by discussing mirror imagery in these novels as tied to the issue of pathological male characters' predominating in the central females' relationships. Some studies, related to mine on a general level, locate the novels' basic thematic movement in a decategorizing or deconstructing of pairs of opposing terms — American/Canadian, culture/nature, male/female, victor/victim, for example. Similar studies are primarily philosophical but not deconstructive and argue that a transformative broadening or heightening of the protagonist's consciousness most thoroughly describes the thematic.[7] Still others treat more textual matters of style, form, or genre.[8]

A strain of criticism that applies to *The Edible Woman* but not to *Surfacing* addresses the novel's interrogation of capitalism. Elizabeth Brady writes that Atwood's "real achievement is to have examined the inter-relationships between the various forms which male domination assumes in a woman's life, and then to have related these forms to the larger domination structure of consumer capitalism." Gayle Greene argues that Marian's doubly obscured position under a menial job and dull fiancé reflects the conditions of many North American women, concluding that "[t]his similarity between woman's position in the alienated world of work and her sexual objectification ... has been the subject of recent marxist-feminist discussion."[9] While Brady's and Greene's readings distinctively give voice to Atwood's leftist and feminist thematic as do very few other interpretations, they do not situate it in specifically Canadian terms.

THE EDIBLE WOMAN

Peter in Atwood's first novel matches exactly Lasch's descriptions of the narcissistic personality as one who "cannot live without an admiring audience" and for whom "the world is a mirror."[10] Peter lives in that "eternal present" Otto Kernberg has associated with pathological narcissism,[11] and Atwood persistently links him not only with mirrors but also with the mirroring device of the camera.

Given no history in the narrative, Peter seems forced to validate himself continually by seeing himself reflected in others, and he needs to marry to gain Marian as a permanently reflecting fixture. Atwood writes of Peter and his one unmarried male friend, Trigger, Peter's companion in machismo, that they "had clutched each other like drowning men, each trying to make the other the reassuring reflection of himself that he needed. Now Trigger had sunk and the mirror would be empty."[12] Peter's eyes themselves become mirrors in which Marian sees herself (83), and his apartment building has a "floor-length mirror" (225). Finally, at Peter's and Marian's engagement party, Peter "raised the camera and aimed it at her" as "his mouth opened in a snarl of teeth" (244). Marian escapes from Peter that night, and on her way out of his apartment, Marian "avoided the mirror" (244).

At the start of the novel, Marian, in turn, is unable to see herself alone and clearly; she relies instead on imposed identities which ultimately cannot satisfy her. Her own relationship with mirrors encodes her ambivalence toward herself and Peter until the text's final pages, and an ambivalence toward other women that lasts throughout. Marian's first encounter with mirrors (other than those associated with Peter) occurs in a dream that her hands and feet are dissolving, that she is disintegrating. She explains that in the dream "I had started towards the mirror to see what was happening to my face, but at that point I woke up" (43), temporarily saving her face, her dwindling self-image.

Marian then undergoes the most significant kind of mirroring experience in Atwood's fiction: she is placed momentarily on the other side of the mirror looking out, in a position of temporary but complete disintegration. Such a state demands that the subject be mirrored not in the conventional way but rather by another person. About to dress for the engagement party late in the novel, Marian glimpses herself in her bedroom mirror, where she appears between two childhood dolls that flank the mirror and gaze out at her:

> She saw herself in the mirror between them for an instant as though she was inside them [the dolls], inside both of them at once, looking out: herself, a vague damp form in a rumpled dress-ing-gown, not quite focused . . . the centre, whatever it was in the glass, the thing that held them together, would soon be quite empty. By the strength of their separate visions they were trying to pull her apart. (219)

Little of the ordinary and sensible young woman remains at this moment, and it is now that she telephones Duncan, the novel's other man and an aimless graduate student, to invite him to her engage-ment party.

Duncan makes clear earlier in the novel that he has deliberately smashed the only mirror in his apartment. He explains to Marian that "I got tired of being afraid I'd walk in there some morning and wouldn't be able to see my own reflection in it. So I went and grabbed the frying-pan out of the kitchen and gave it a whack" (139). He calls his action "a perfectly understandable symbolic narcissistic gesture" (139), meaning in this context that he hoped to preserve some of his faded self-image by not allowing it to be abducted in a mirror. His defensive gesture can be called progressively narcissistic in that it allows him, through the ensuing relationship with Marian, to explore the possibility of a renewed identity. Marian and Duncan become for a crucial time — for a kind of mirror stage — speaking images of one another and talk themselves into necessary change.

The critical place reached by Atwood's central women, and less emphatically by some of her men, is an inability to tolerate the con-ventional self-images, coded to mirrors, that a narcissistic culture offers. Still, the reclamation of the history of Canadian women remains inaccessible to Marian; her perceptions of her gender remain troubled, as is clear in her meditations at the office party when her engagement is announced. Marian is a market researcher in an office comprised mainly of married women who study the shopping tastes of other married women and whose careers are going nowhere. About her co-workers she thinks:

> She looked around the room at all the women there, at the mouths opening and shutting, to talk or to eat. Here, sitting like any other group of women at an afternoon feast, they no longer had the varnish of officialdom that separated them, during regular office hours, from the vast anonymous ocean of housewives whose minds they were employed to explore. They could have been wearing housecoats and curlers. ... They were ripe, some rapidly becoming overripe, some already beginning to shrivel ... in various stages of growth and decay. ...
>
> She examined the women's bodies with interest, critically, as though she had never seen them before. And in a way she hadn't. ... What peculiar creatures they were; and the continual flux between the outside and the inside, taking things in, giving them out, chewing, words, potato-chips, burps, grease, hair, babies, milk, excrement, cookies, vomit, coffee, tomato-juice, blood, tea, sweat, liquor, tears, and garbage. ...
>
> ... At some time she would be — or no, already she was like that too; she was one of them, her body the same, identical, merged with that other flesh that choked the air in the flowered room with its sweet organic scent; she felt suffocated by this thick sargasso-sea of femininity. ... [S]he wanted something solid, clear; a man; she wanted Peter. (166-167)

Peter, however, "suffocates" her in his own way, and she rejects him, at the same time rejecting conventional marriage and her place in the "merging" of flesh that would make her indistinguishable from all other women. While Marian's power at the end of this novel seems both lonely and harsh — narcissistic — it is mitigated by Duncan's presence. An alliance with him at least keeps Marian from safe confinement as a Toronto society housewife (rather like the later, less fortunate figures of Joan Foster's mother in *Lady Oracle*, Elizabeth's Auntie Muriel in *Life Before Man*, and the dreaded Mrs. Smeath in *Cat's Eye*, all Torontonians).

With the less conventional Duncan in their cheap hotel room near the novel's end, Marian can begin to see herself, though faintly, "in the yellowed wavery glass of the bathroom mirror" (256), signalling for her an emergent, independent sense of self. Later that day in her apartment, readying herself for the confrontation with Peter, quite dramatically "she grinned into the mirror, showing her teeth" (268). Marian in this dubiously favourable mirroring seems at least to incorporate a role that is not conventionally feminine. And Duncan, who joins her as she re-establishes a relationship with food, never seems quite conventionally masculine somehow because unemployed and associated throughout with the "women's" work of washing and ironing clothes. Futile and directionless as their eccentricity seems, both figures escape the ordinary; they have avoided the Canada of small-town Ontario as Marian describes it in the passage below. With her engagement, her parents'

> fears about the effects of her university education, never stated but always apparent, had been calmed at last. They had probably been worried she would turn into a high school teacher or a maiden aunt or a dope addict or a female executive, or that she would undergo some shocking physical transformation, like developing muscles and a deep voice or growing moss. She could picture their anxious consultations over cups of tea. (174)

While Marian's and Duncan's relationship remains vaguely defined, it at least represents a freeing change from rigid bourgeois conventionality. Duncan's place as a man capable of the first step in progressive narcissism is significant because it establishes what will be a recurrent movement in Atwood's work: a return to selected male figures in her texts to reclaim them. The goal of progressive narcissism is to enable her women to empower not only themselves but also others, often the men they love. This mutual enabling will, with increasing clarity, link Atwood's feminism with her quasi-socialism.

SURFACING

A more sustained critique of pathological narcissism than *The Edible Woman, Surfacing* still represents the central female primarily in her relationships with men and with women she hardly knows. The narrator's mirroring experiences resemble Marian's but surpass them in that they involve the journey back to women she does know well. Mirrors in *Surfacing* have received critical comment, but not in connection with the influential men in the narrator's experience. Criticism also does not name and explicate masculinist narcissism but rather treats thematic issues of decategorization or deconstruction,[13] transformations of consciousness,[14] and more literary matters of style and form.[15] My reading presents an interpretation of the precise value of the narrator's late turn to her mother as the start of a crucial process in Atwood's work with language, and is as such most closely related to Sally Robinson's essay, which states: "the fact that Atwood's protagonist links her other language with the recovery of her mother suggests that it is close to Kristeva's semiotic."[16]

To look back to the cultural milieu corresponding to *The Edible Woman* and then forward to *Surfacing,* I suggest that Peter, with his staid occupation and predictable male diversions, serves two purposes: the first is to caricature Canadian men who try uncritically and unsuccessfully to adopt an identity from other cultural ideologies, and the second is to set him in place as a recurring character in Atwood's texts, a man who will become easily recognized and will always appear as obstacle to the search by Atwood's other, more sympathetic characters for less artificial selves. Duncan, on the other hand, stands for the brooding, confused Canadian man who chooses to live with no clear identity rather than one that is imported, a decision that leaves him open to change. Duncan's kind of character also reappears in Atwood's texts. By the year 1972, when *Surfacing* was published, cultural upheaval in both Canada and the United States had called traditional mores into question and, as if in response, Atwood begins to look more urgently for solutions through her female characters.

Atwood does not yet, however, achieve the sustained political statement in *Surfacing* that she will in later texts, detailing Canadian women's power, because the narrator dwells too exclusively on her identity in relation to men. But at a critical period late in the novel, the narrator turns the cabin mirror to the wall in her wilderness hideout to prepare herself for the appearance of her mother's nurturing spirit. Atwood's focus on the narrator vis-à-vis men, and on other women and men in relationships, is consistent with Atwood's ultimate project: to revise the categories according to which North Americans accede to identity. She will proceed from *Surfacing*, however, to place women in relations with other women more exclusively in the mirror stage of her production overall. This text somewhat haltingly initiates the stage.

Because men dominate in the narrator's coming to identity, it is important to understand each of the significant male characters with reference to his entrapment in pathological narcissism, his "Americanization." In order of their relative pathology, from greatest to least, they are; her current lover's colleague David, her former lover and art teacher, her current lover, her brother, and her father. The one male character apparently free of narcissism is minor, her father's friend Paul. The significant women in the narrator's quest are her "best friend" [17] Anna, whose effect on the narrator is too negligible to warrant commentary, her mother's friend Madame (Paul's wife), and her mother.

A narcissistic male will choose a woman who reflects his image becomingly, although he knows such an image masks his real fears and doubts. Yet he continues in contemptuous dependence upon any who will supply his lack, and the power he exerts over whomever he can is desperate, manipulative, and tinged with loathing both for himself and for his victims.

I suggest that the narrator's own sense of disconnection with her past results from her intimacy with men who suffer in varying degrees from pathological narcissism. Only when she can glimpse a female ethos represented by her Canadian mother can the narrator find a way around the males' confusion. As she explains, she is searching for something lost, "for something I could recognize as myself" (109), "the missing part of me" (129). The search hinges on her relationship with her parents and is interrupted when she becomes her teacher's mistress, briefly carries their child, and agrees to an abortion. After the abortion she declares, "I couldn't go there, home, I never went there again, I sent them a postcard" (169); she gives as her reason her parents' "perilous innocence" (169), a quality she sees as opposed to the will to control. Later, rejecting her lover and denying the abortion, the narrator remains suspended between identities until she confronts her own power late in the novel.

Even more narcissistic than her first lover is one of her companions on her island quest, her current lover Joe's colleague David. A communications teacher, David is garrulous indeed; late in the novel, the narrator sees David clearly for the first time as a man who "didn't know what language to use, he'd forgotten his own, he had to copy. Secondhand American was spreading over him in patches" (178). David might, however, more accurately be called a failed Canadian in the narrator's terms because when younger he had attempted, as a student of theology, the very spiritual quest she now enters on. His disillusionment propels him into politics, where he assumes a correct Canadian nationalist position but defines Canada simplistically as that which is not the United States, a definition that his own actions in any case betray. David seems most certainly "American" in a stereotypical sense — predatory and ruthless — in his treatment of his wife Anna, and yet Anna confides in the narrator that David "likes to make me cry because he can't do it himself" (145). Having repressed his vulnerability, his ability to feel, David — like the narrator herself — has "forgotten his own" language.

A character who previously manipulated the narrator in the way that David manipulates Anna is the narrator's art teacher, her first lover. She reveals:

> For him I could have been anyone but for me he was unique, the first, that's where I learned. I worshipped him, non-child-bride, idolater, I kept the scraps of his handwriting like saints' relics, he

never wrote letters, all I had was the criticisms in red pencil he paperclipped to my drawings. C's and D's, he was an idealist, he said he didn't want our relationship as he called it to influence aesthetic judgment. He didn't want our relationship to influence anything; it was to be kept separate from life. A certificate framed on the wall, his proof that he was still young. (174)

While the narrator can believe that her lover "imposed" (39) the fetus on her, she can also be his "idolater" in a position clearly victimized. With wife and children already, he never offers the narrator marriage and finally leaves her, strictly controlling their affair from beginning to end.

Her current lover, Joe, is linked by his occupation to her first lover; a potter, Joe also attempts to control the narrator. She reads his marriage proposal as yet another move in a power struggle demanding her submission so that for him it can be "a victory, some flag [he] can wave, parade [he] can have in [his] head" (104). Although she comes to feel that she can and wants to save him in the specific way she has been saved, she first recognizes his neurosis as narcissistic. "[H]e didn't love me," she sees, "it was an idea of himself he loved and he wanted someone to join him, anyone would do, I didn't matter so I didn't have to care" (130-131). But until Joe confronts his own failures — his wavering between self-hatred because his pots "don't sell at all" (66) and an arrogant "claim to superior artistic seriousness" (66) — the narrator cannot possibly supply him with a "worthy idea of himself." His undue reliance upon the narrator's need for him, his envy of her success, and his mercurial self-esteem mark him as pathologically narcissistic. And yet the narrator chooses him as mate and father of her child.

By contrast with his colleague, David, Joe's saving feature is his taciturnity. As the narrator observes, "what will preserve him is the absence of words" (186). Guessing that "for him I am the entrance" (172), the narrator will presumably attempt to bring Joe to the new language she searches for, that in which the meaning of power might be revised to include the power to acknowledge innocence, failure, and loss — all that Joe has repressed to preserve a threatened and threatening masculinity — a power different from that associated with the novel's Americanized characters.

Moving back into the narrator's past, it seems clear that her relationship with her brother creates the pattern for her connection with her first lover in that in both cases she fears, loathes, and is in awe of their power. When young, she frees the live creatures in her brother's "laboratory" (155) in a compassionate gesture and then, faced with his anger, grows too frightened to do so ever again, concluding that "[b]ecause of my fear they were killed" (155). She later realizes that she could similarly have protected her fetus against the controlling intelligence of her lover, but her entrapment in males' self-images, and so in their desperate narcissistic powers of manipulation and domination, prevents her. She is incapable of self-motivated action as long as she allows herself to be defined exclusively in relation to men, and insofar as those men are afflicted with pathological narcissism, her actions become as menacing as theirs.

Her alliance with such men has always been close and meaningful. The narrator's Canadian father has repressed his faith and his feeling, like the text's Americanized men, leaving the pursuit of what is not logical to his wife. As a child the narrator worships him. She tells us that "[m]y father explained everything but my mother never did" (86). Her chief complaint about her father, however, is precisely that he claimed extraordinary power without subjecting the term "power" itself to analysis, giving his daughter an incomplete sense of what it means to mature. "If you tell your children God doesn't exist," she explains, "they will be forced to believe you are the god" (124). And "God" becomes very much a part of the nature which was her father's life as an entomologist; it is to nature she retreats. In her underwater encounter with the "dark oval trailing limbs" (167), she begins her reunion with her past and recognizes that the power she begins to feel is linked to the spirits of nature, "the only [gods] who had ever given me anything I needed; and freely" (170). But her father and his gods are finally exposed, and his legacy to her is one of "reparation" (218): "He realized he was an intruder; the cabin, the fences, the fires and paths were violations; now his own fence excludes him, as logic excludes love" (218). The narrator feels released from the study of her physical place of origin because of the visitation of her father's spirit, though she has yet to understand her parents' messages fully.

Occupying a unique position in the text is the least American and pathologically narcissistic of its male characters, the aging French-Canadian villager, Paul, a man admired by the narrator's father for living "the simple life" (27). Rooted in his culture and knowing immediate connections with his past and future, Paul survives not by speaking — his first language is in fact unintelligible to the Americans — but with his hands. Although the narrator has little to do with Paul directly, he and his wife seem to have become associated in her mind with the figurines at their home, the "barometer couple in their wooden house, enshrined in their niche on Paul's front porch, my ideal" (163), an emblem throughout *Surfacing* of the peace and balance the narrator searches for,[18] an integration of past with present, male with female. And Paul is significant, too, not only for being linked in his lack of narcissism and his silence with the narrator's mother but also for providing the only commentary on the mother apart from the narrator's. He assures the narrator early in the novel that her mother "was a good woman" (25).

The narrator's mother is her husband's opposite and is repeatedly associated with the nature he tried to dominate. His is an exclusively logical, mathematical, scientific attitude, whereas hers goes beyond ordinary language. Unreflective in her faithful journal-keeping, the narrator's mother is represented much more through imagery than is her father, with his charts and maxims, and her mother must be read through processes of poetic association rather than logical sequence, recalling the Kristevan "semiotic activity" associated with dream work. She is linked to Kristeva's theory of poetic language, too, because her radical Canadianness also represents an ethic subversive of Americanization.

Atwood's poetic language here, that used to describe the mother, is markedly different from the language used to describe narcissistic men. First, all of the narrator's most vivid memories of her mother ally her not with human nature but with birds, the most strategically placed natural figures in this text. In an early memory of her mother scaring away a bear, the narrator describes her as having "arms upraised as though she was flying ... as if she knew a foolproof magic formula: gesture and word" (95). Then, on her deathbed, "[s]he was very thin ... skin tight over her curved beak nose, hands on the sheet curled like bird claws clinging to a perch" (25). And in the final vision of her mother, she is indistinguishable from the jays she had always so carefully tended (213-214).

Structured by loon cries, as Charlotte Walker Mendez argues,[19] *Surfacing* also dwells upon herons, one of them hanged by the Americanized Canadian male hunters. These birds are in turn figurally associated with the narrator's mother. Poetic logic overtakes the narrator as she prepares for the first time to dive for the rock paintings to which her father's drawings lead her. She recalls in language quite different from that which the narrator earlier uses to analyze men:

> The shape of the heron flying above us the first evening we fished, legs and neck stretched, wings outspread, a blue-gray cross, and the other heron or was it the same one, hanging wrecked from the tree. Whether it died willingly, consented, whether Christ died willingly, anything that suffers and dies instead of us is Christ; if they didn't kill birds and fish they would have killed us. The animals die that we may live. ... But we refuse to worship; the body worships with blood and muscle but the thing in the knob head will not, wills not to, the head is greedy, it consumes but does not give thanks.(164-165)

With a "they" and "us" opposition in place, the narrator begins to study and ally herself with "us," victims, such as her mute Canadian mother and the hanged heron. The centre of what she must learn "to worship" shifts to what "suffers and dies instead of us." Her aborted fetus, the heron, her mother as nature, and Christ all become such victims in the narrator's imagination, figures she comes to see as killed not by inevitable processes of a natural law outside of her control but by human "will" and "greed," including her own. Her mother, who suffered crippling headaches throughout the narrator's memory of her, dies of brain cancer; while the narrator cannot be held responsible for her mother's death, she is conscious nevertheless of having abandoned her mother and aborted the grandchild she felt her parents wanted. She allowed her lover's will to prevail and repressed her own identification with the fetus.

In allying herself with victims, the narrator can then see her mother more clearly: in terms of how she is presented in the novel and what she represents, the narrator's mother contrasts with all of the men in *Surfacing*, and most sharply with those who are most narcissistic. Theirs is a will to dominate, hers a will to tolerate; their concerns are political, hers mystical; they are obsessed with the encroachment of language as defined by Americans, while she is silent; they need their egos shored up, and she disregards hers. The mother's very ethereality supplies what the narrator needs to balance the paternal values of defence and reason; the mother stands for that maternal history that Atwood's women will rediscover in the mirror stage of her work, a history which, in its obscurity, matches Canada's own.[20]

The mirror stage in *Surfacing* itself comes near the end, after the narrator has determined "to be more careful about my memories, I have to be sure they're my own and not the memories of other people telling me what I felt, how I acted, what I said" (84). As in the mirror stage (as I define it in Chapter One) the subject must be disposed to change, specifically to learn or relearn language and in that way accede to a more or less stable but still limited self. She will then find in other adults ego ideals she recognizes and accepts as her own and will adopt their speech in a therapeutic narcissism. Because the ego ideal is Canadian, so is the subject following the mirror stage.

Between the narrator's turning the cabin mirror to the wall (205) and then turning it back (222), she experiences the vision of her mother as bird and her father as wolf (218) and fish (219), resulting finally in the narrator's ability to go on with a newly tempered sense of self. She initiates the process of recovery with the telling statement, "I must stop being in the mirror" (205). From her father at this crucial time she seems to gain intellectual humility, an understanding that nature is a mystery that can neither be penetrated and overcome nor ignored, and from her mother she learns acceptance of vulnerability or emotional modesty, both the awe of nature and the vulnerability truer somehow to the Canadian than to the American mythos. But the critical effect of a successful mirror stage is not only perceptual but also verbal: the narrator must be able to articulate her new relation to the world.

The narrator's particular semantic concern in *Surfacing* is with power and what she initially conceives to be its opposite, innocence; roughly, Americans have power and Canadians are innocent of it, an opposition Atwood herself holds responsible for a dangerous Canadian reticence.[21] The narrator confides that as a small child she believed the seeds inside bean pods would make her "all-powerful" if she ate them, and that she later experimented with this hypothesis and "it didn't work. Just as well, I think, as I had no idea what I would do with the power once I got it; if I'd turned out like the others with power I would have been evil" (43).

Her World War II childhood, extending the power/innocence opposition beyond North America, poses Hitler as a devil, as evil incarnate, whose antithesis in the narrator's childish imagination is the Christ of the neighbouring French-Canadian Catholics. But even as a child she hoped to be rid of the danger of thinking categorically when she drew the picture that late in the novel becomes the signal from her mother. The girlish drawing shows a woman pregnant with the narrator and "a man with horns on his head like cow horns and a barbed tail"; she explains that "the man was God, I'd drawn him when my brother learned in the winter about the Devil and God: if the Devil was allowed a tail and horns, God needed them also, they were advantages" (185). Innocence must be joined to power to redefine both, in other words, as the young girl knows and as the grown narrator must rediscover.

What, specifically, the narrator achieves on her island quest is a renewed sense of power, as the many uses of the word in the novel's second and third sections witness. And the power that her search for the island gods restores her to derives in the end precisely from her parents' influence, especially her mother's — the influence that she had avoided in her years of submission to a series of troubled men. Her final resolve speaks for itself as thematic summary, and it is significantly inscribed in a speculative, self-reflexive, and emotionally candid mode quite the opposite of the spare and noncommittal language with which this novel opens:

> [B]ack to the city and the pervasive menace, the Americans. They exist, they're advancing, they must be dealt with, but possibly they can be watched and predicted and stopped without being copied.
>
> No gods to help me now, they're questionable once more, theoretical as Jesus. They've receded, back to the past, inside the skull, is it the same place. They'll never appear to me again, I can't afford it; from now on I'll have to live in the usual way, defining them by their absence; and love by its failures, power by its loss, its renunciation. I regret them; but they give only one kind of truth, one hand.
>
> No total salvation, resurrection, Our father, Our mother, I pray, Reach down for me, but it won't work: they dwindle, grow, become what they were, human. Something I never gave them credit for; but their totalitarian innocence was my own. (221)

Defining power by its renunciation means precisely a reclamation of innocence, a condition that refuses evil. The power of the "Americans," a particularly narcissistic power in its will to control, gives way not to powerlessness — the narrator states clearly that she must relinquish "the old belief that I am powerless" (222) — but to the will to "trust" (224). Obsessions with ego strength, associated with the Americans in *Surfacing*, are displaced by faith in a process by which Canadians return to and study their history to discover in it what is distinctively theirs. The narrator accepts her rescuer, Joe, because "he isn't an American, I can see that now; he isn't anything, he is only half formed, and for that reason I can trust him" (224).[22]

The mirror stage in Atwood's second novel anticipates the process as it occurs in *Lady Oracle* and *Two-Headed Poems*, but it fails to enact it fully because male figures play a too significant role in *Surfacing*. The mother's legacy, the feminist part of the emerging progressive narcissism in Atwood's work, remains suggested rather than explicit. Although the goal in Atwood's work is consistently a reclamation of both sides of the pairs of opposites structuring her texts — American/Canadian, male/female, culture/nature, evil/good, power/victimage, capitalist/socialist — ultimately complete social renewal, in other words, the goal cannot be reached, if it can be reached at all, until the second term gains prominence and receives sustained attention. This occurs when Canadian women dominate in two of Atwood's central texts. But her feminism must always be seen, even in the midst of her women's mirror stage, as part of an encompassing project. For as feminism gains momentum historically in North America, Atwood champions its successes and then begins to chronicle the challenges and attacks upon feminism labelled backlash.

❖

Chapter Three

MOTHERING:
LADY ORACLE AND
TWO-HEADED POEMS

IN THE MIRROR STAGE of Atwood's writing, it is no longer the powerful narcissistic men who affect the central female characters but rather Canadian women, like the narrator's mother in *Surfacing*. The influential women in these mid- to late-1970s' texts are related to the female characters by blood; their hold on the younger women thus reaches farther back in time and is more lasting. And this very influence has been what the younger women have had to repress to enter a man's world.

Joan Foster's aunt and mother in *Lady Oracle* (1976) and the persona's female ancestors, daughter, and sister in *Two-Headed Poems* (1978) represent the difficult but inevitable legacy of the younger protagonists: difficult because it is muted, hard for them to understand, and therefore frightening to the young women who aspire to the freedoms offered by a growing feminist movement in their milieux; and inevitable because it comprises the history of which Atwood's female characters are a product, the same history their narcissistic lovers in their Americanization failed to see. As her central women discover their maternal forebears they begin to introduce their resilient voices into the production of Canadian culture.

The politicized persona of Atwood's central females is discovered not in *Two-Headed Poems*, however, where the voice is developed, but in *Lady Oracle* as its protagonist comes to name and value not only the gentle goodness of her beloved Aunt Lou but also her mother's high and completely frustrated critical intelligence. It is as though two strains of recent Canadian women's history must be joined to create what is, for Joan Foster, the right progressively narcissistic identity, one both compassionate and demanding. *Lady Oracle* prepares for *Two-Headed Poems* in that way, much as Atwood's first novel enables the second.

In a 1978 interview, Atwood hints that her feminism and her explicit political critiques will begin to appear clearly and merge in the late 1970s: "in my most recent poems, I seem to be less concerned about the relationships between men and women than I am about those among women (grandmother-mother-daughter, sisters) and those between cultures."[1] Although she refers here only to her poetry, her comments on *Lady Oracle* show that it, too, is given to "relationships ... among women" and so implicitly to Atwood's growing political commitment. She states that "*Lady Oracle* ... is all about mother-figures. The whole book is about that. ... *Lady Oracle* is a search for 'the real mother.'"[2]

Criticism of *Lady Oracle* gives considerable attention to issues of feminist psychoanalysis[3] and mirroring[4] and makes mention of Canadian nationalism,[5] language,[6] and the distinguishing features of Atwood's men;[7] it is dominated, however, by a generic approach, endorsed by Atwood's own comment that the novel is "anti-gothic." Atwood's assessment in turn connects this text with her feminist historiography in that Joan's successful search for her mother's empowering legacy reverses the plot of modern Gothic in which women, particularly mothers and daughters, remain mutually antagonistic.[8]

LADY ORACLE

As important as Joan Delacourt Foster's avoidance of the Gothic plot is her escape from regressively narcissistic men, an escape more dramatic and final than Marian's in *The Edible Woman* or even *Surfacing's* narrator, perhaps because Joan's entanglement with such men is more permanent and demands stronger measures. Like Atwood's earlier protagonists, Joan finds release in a lover who is more "Canadian" (in this case an anglophile Canadian poet), but unlike them she is married to an Americanized man throughout the narrative. As the novel opens, Joan has planned and faked her own death to avoid a blackmailer who would reveal to her husband her lover, her career as writer of romance novels, and her childhood obesity. She hides away in the small Italian town of Terremoto where the novel is set.

Joan's occupation as romance writer is one she fears her husband would not take seriously; in that way she is in as vulnerable a position as the market researcher and illustrator before her in Atwood's novels. The pathological narcissism of Joan's husband, Arthur Foster, has kept Joan so fearful that she suppresses her several identities: to Arthur, Joan as readers come to know her hardly exists. We see Arthur, in turn, pass through his own series of identities — among them pamphleteer in a British Ban the Bomb movement, US civil rights activist, writer for a Canadian nationalist tabloid — all of which fail to supply him with an acceptable sense of self. Joan realizes that he "was very good at respecting people's minds, initially. But he would always manage to find some flaw, some little corner of dry rot."[9]

Arthur then experiences a growing contempt, disillusionment, and apathy. Cut off, too, from ties to home and parents, Arthur is unable to form an intimate bond with Joan and remains isolated. She explains that "[n]o matter what I did, Arthur was bound to despise me. I could never be what he wanted" (247); Arthur "didn't trust me" (230); "It took me a while to realize that Arthur enjoyed my defeats. They cheered him up" (210).

Arthur's pathology results from an inability to interact with the dominant order effectively, perhaps reflecting his sense that Canada's historical ties with the parent country, England, have been severed, yet a working alliance with the United States has not been acceptably formed. Separated from his past and with no distinct and purposeful future, Arthur's desperate search for an adequate sense of self cannot, unfortunately, send him to his wife for guidance: as rigidly conventionally male, Arthur is unwilling to look to Joan for help, and she, entangled as she is in self-deception, is incapable of offering it. Still, Joan insists throughout the novel that she loves Arthur, and soon after her successful escape from him she communicates with him by mail, suggesting that she hopes to reunite.

But Joan's search is given much less to understanding the men than the women who have influenced her. With her Aunt Lou, for example — a shaping force in her life — Joan regularly attends 1940s' and 1950s' Hollywood movies, and with Lou and Lou's married lover, Joan also takes part in spiritualist meetings conducted by another of the text's recurring powerful women, the Reverend Leda Sprott. Aunt Lou provides, with the willing of money on the condition that her niece lose 100 pounds, Joan's means of escape from home.

Aunt Lou, Joan's early mother-imago, educates her niece in matters of the heart and represents characteristics opposite to those of Joan's mother, Fran, a woman caught in conventionality. Fran herself explains the difference between the two women, saying of Aunt Lou, "she's good-hearted but she just doesn't care what kind of an impression she makes" (86). Aunt Lou declares to Joan by way of self-analysis, "[t]hat's just the way I am. ... If other people can't handle it, that's their problem. Remember that, dear. You can't always choose your life, but you can learn to accept it" (88). Having married at nineteen a man seven years older and a compulsive gambler, because "[s]he was madly in love with him ... he was tall, dark and handsome" (80), Aunt Lou is abandoned by her husband and provides a model of fatalistic emotional vulnerability which is, for her niece, both appealing and dangerous.

Fran, in contrast, cares primarily about "what kind of impression she makes" and never grows to accept her life. Joan describes her as "an anxious, prudish adult" (46), "too intense to be likable" (180), with "a hawk's eye for anything out of place" (66), "menacing and cold" (214). Very much like Joan's teenage confidantes who trade their potential for the promised security of conventional marriage, Fran "had made her family her career as she had been told to do, and look at us: a sulky fat slob of a daughter and a husband who wouldn't talk to her"; Joan adds, "I and my father had totally failed to justify her life the way she felt it should have been justified" (178).

From these two characters arose Joan's identity, an identity suspended between opposites: a part of Joan is given to romantic indulgences while another favours duplicity and self-denial. Early in Joan's remembering, Aunt Lou seems the more obvious influence in that Joan takes the name Louisa K. Delacourt as the pseudonym under which she writes the Costume Gothics. More, Joan seems to use the pattern of Aunt Lou's eccentric life to shape her Gothic heroines, career women of a kind who lure away other women's husbands and find a shaky happiness. Perhaps reflecting upon her mother, too, Joan divulges that "[i]n my books all wives [like Fran Delacourt] were eventually either mad or dead, or both" (319). And so Joan's private life as a writer has always been devoted to remembering her female ancestors, and that process merely becomes her primary occupation in Terremoto.

As Joan begins to examine her past during her time in Italy, she believes that she has excised all connections with her mother and attempts to show that her decisions have been based on the example of Aunt Lou. As *Lady Oracle* ends, however, she dramatically reverses that pattern and acknowledges her likeness to her mother. Fran had "run away from home at age sixteen and never gone back" (68), Joan notes. Joan too leaves home as a teenager, setting in place for both women recurring strategies of evasion. Near the novel's end, Joan muses, "I might as well face it ... I was an artist, an escape artist" (334). And on the novel's last page, Joan implies that she has at least started to understand the emotional hold over her of both Aunt Lou and her mother, by first relinquishing her Aunt Lou persona and then accepting as invaluably useful her mother's strong will. She resolves: "I won't write any more Costume Gothics ... I think they were bad for me. ... I keep thinking I should learn some lesson from all of this, as my mother would have said" (345). By borrowing Fran's firm resolve, trying to accept the lessons of her past, Joan begins to claim and activate her mother's influence.

Together, the lives of Louisa K. and Fran Delacourt trace in a broad outline examples of recent histories of ordinary middle-class Canadian women: Louisa as self-supporting but in a position with only narrow authority, and Fran as a conventional housewife. In that way, they pose to Joan irreconcilable alternatives — "You could dance, or you could have the love of a good man" (335) — unless she can somehow incorporate the best of each woman's influence. While she had lived out the effects of Aunt Lou's occupation and attitudes, writing for "at least a hundred thousand people ... among them ... the mothers of the nation" (247), giving them "hope ... a vision of a better world" (35), she tires of the world of romance and turns back throughout her days alone in Italy to the mother she rejected. A half-believer in the astral projection Leda Sprott preached, Joan senses that her mother's spirit has haunted her since Fran's death and, during her mother's last appearance to her, Joan wonders, in a complete reversal of her first hateful comments upon Fran, "could she see I loved her? ... I longed to console her. ... I would do what she wanted" (329).

What Joan learns at her Italian retreat is that by redeeming her past she can accept herself and, perhaps, inherit those "great powers" that the spiritual mentor Leda Sprott twice instructs her that she possesses (112, 206). Understanding her own power might further — by a stretch of the imagination — allow Joan to empower others, which would thus serve the developing "socialist" goal of successful identity formation or progressive narcissism in Atwood's writing. For Canadian left-nationalism ensures "a more distinct, compassionate character than its neighbour," the United States, according to Lawrence Martin,[10] and Joan, although she does not know her own mind well enough to perceive this, is enabled, precisely because of her aunt's benevolent influence, to accept her responsibility to others. That ability is made public in *Lady Oracle* when Joan publishes her first book in her own name, a book of poems whose central character is Joan's mother.

The Reverend Leda Sprott and Atwood herself clarify what Joan cannot, that the personal history from which she escaped and from which her marriage has continued to separate her in fact produced an able person, one worth Joan's getting to know. Atwood, in an interview published in 1987, praises Joan as "the most amiable" of all her characterizations.[11] Leda Sprott too appraises Joan highly, stating on the day of her wedding to Arthur that "[p]eople have faith in you ... they trust you" (206). Joan herself is able to feel compassion for and devotion to her audience of women readers, the same kind of women who, as 1950s' teenagers, confided to her their quests for male approval and who now simply need "to escape" (34) within her Costume Gothics.

Joan's misery, resulting from a failed relationship with her mother in childhood and early adulthood, seems, in fact, to leave her especially sensitive to others' pain (though such misery can have an opposite psychological effect, as other Atwoodian characters show). "I empathize with anything in pain" (92), she claims — importantly, in the end, even her mother's pain. She states directly that her sympathies lie with people on whom "[l]ife had been hard ... and they had not fought back, they'd collapsed like soufflés in a high wind. Escape wasn't a luxury for them, it was a necessity" (34). Whereas Arthur's male narcissism imprisons him in an endless round of "theories and ideologies" (35), Joan's lack of fulfilling narcissistic experiences of any kind threatens to fate her to a career as "a sentimentalist ... of the sloppiest kind" (14), until she extends the process begun by the protagonists of *The Edible Woman* and *Surfacing* and comes to know herself and Canadian women's history more thoroughly than they. She must learn to value her compassion for others, although she may never act upon that compassion in the novel.

MIRRORS IN THE MIRROR STAGE

In *Lady Oracle*, Joan's reclamation of her mother's legacy is obviously coded to Atwood's use of mirror imagery, and by that means the process and results of progressive narcissism gain definition. Joan's mother is caught in conventional positioning and therefore in the literal figure of the mirror. In order to break the hold of regressive narcissism for herself and for Joan, she must show another, more authentic self which Joan can accept as influential. As a girl, Joan watches her mother applying cosmetics in front of a three-panelled mirror and realizes that "[i]nstead of making her happier, these sessions appeared to make her sadder, as if she saw behind or within the mirror some fleeting image she was unable to capture or duplicate" (66). Then, to initiate the automatic writing which produces her first work published under her own name as a mature woman, Joan "lit the candle end and set it in front of my dressing-table mirror. (I'd recently bought a three-sided one, like my mother's.)" (219). Eventually "[t]here was movement at the edge of the mirror. I gasped and turned around. Surely there had been a figure, standing behind me" (220). Fran's "fleeting image" from Joan's youth survives and becomes the central figure in the "Lady Oracle" poems; Fran replaces Aunt Lou as heroine of Joan's fictions. The nonrealistic mode of this scene and its interchange between mother and daughter harks back to the narrator's mystical reunion with her mother in *Surfacing*.

As the new heroine of her daughter's "Lady Oracle" poems, poems that make Joan a Canadian star, Fran "lived under the earth somewhere. ... She was enormously powerful, almost like a goddess, but it was an unhappy power. ... [C]ertainly she had nothing to do with me. ... I was happy. Happy and inept" (222). Only after Joan's communion with and acknowledgement of the spectral figure of her "enormously powerful" mother can she begin to admit that Aunt Lou's legacy of romantic happiness no longer satisfies her. Aunt Lou, Joan states, "was certainly generous" (88), and yet after Joan has freed her mother's spirit from the mirror, displacing Aunt Lou somewhat, she recognizes that "[m]y ability to give was limited, I was not inexhaustible. I was not serene, not really. I wanted things, for myself" (253). Louisa's instructions in charity, romance, and faith need to be tempered, it seems, with the "unhappy power" of ambition and pride represented by Joan's mother, whose relationship with Joan in place of a career "was professionalised early. She was to be the manager ... I was to be the product" (67). More revealingly, Joan muses of her mother,

[i]t wasn't that she was aggressive and ambitious, although she was both these things. Perhaps she wasn't aggressive or ambitious enough. If she'd ever decided what she really wanted to do and had gone out and done it, she wouldn't have seen me as a reproach to her, the embodiment of her own failure and depression. (67)

To reach her greatest efficacy, Joan must "decide[] what she really want[s] to do and [go] out and [do] it," a project that seems clearly to entail joining the two strands of women's history represented by Aunt Lou's futile gentleness and Fran's imprisoned strength. Joan's empowered, compassionate self should rid the Fran persona of her unbecoming, conventional roles as wife and mother and provide the Aunt Lou imago with a spark of wilfulness. The point of forming such a new self, in turn, is to challenge the pathology represented most obviously in this text by the figure of Joan's husband, Arthur. And Joan does plan to return to Toronto, reunite with her husband, and announce her various identities.

TWO-HEADED POEMS

What Arthur and his colleagues at their left-nationalist Canadian magazine ironically fear most in *Lady Oracle* becomes, in fact, the goal of Atwood's speaker in *Two-Headed Poems*, popularizing an anti-American consciousness. Whereas Arthur shows "alarm" as a left-nationalist ideology gains public credence because, to his mind, "the revolution was getting into the wrong hands" (266), the speaker in Atwood's first explicitly political work (certainly "the wrong hands" in Arthur Foster's view) attempts to find a revolutionary North American language. It is as though Joan's empowered identity speaks up in this volume; narcissistic men appear less often (but highly strategically) to be replaced by the voices of thinking Canadian women.

Here "poetic language" appears, that which for Kristeva represents a subversion of ordinary grammatical structures and so of the larger economic and sociopolitical structures they support. For example,

Atwood's speaker uses vulgar diction for the first time in her work, with the intention of affronting capitalist-imperialist Americans and their Canadian accomplices. In this text Atwood achieves the most coherent and energetic expression of a Canadian poetics both socialist and feminist, even as she implicitly comments on the tradition of Canadian poetry with which she is allied. "I would say that the influences on my novels are more international than the influences on my poetry," she states. "I learned poetry from Canadian poets."[12]

The fact that in this book of poems she uses vulgar language links the volume, tenuously, with Kristeva's early theories in, for example, *Desire in Language*, referred to in Chapter One. Atwood, whose poetic voice had previously used only conventional language, however acerbic its tone, breaks with her own traditional personae and thus with normal diction and sound, thereby introducing the "poetic economy" Kristeva describes as "coupled with crises of social institutions (state, family, religion)" in our time.[13] But I would argue that Atwood's project and Kristeva's concept can in fact be seen to mirror one another further if one refers to Atwood's defence of the subversiveness, in North American culture, of a plain poetic style. Poetic language is distinguished not by its difference from ordinary speech but conversely by its likeness to it in a culture valuing an odd or original style. And in any case, Kristeva has generalized her view of what constitutes subversive, poetic language in the years since her *Revolution in Poetic Language* (see Chapter One).

Atwood writes:

> In some countries, an author is censored not only for what he says but for how he says it. An unconventional style is therefore a declaration of artistic freedom. Here we are eclectic, we don't mind experimental styles; in fact, we devote learned journals to their analysis; but our critics sneer at anything they consider 'heavy social commentary' or — a worse word — 'message.' Stylistic heavy guns are dandy, as long as they aren't pointed anywhere in particular.

Her reasoning here suggests that the combination of plain style and "message" in *Two-Headed Poems* is subversive of the tastes of bourgeois

North America, just as the experimental style Kristeva values subverts in other conditions. Atwood's decision to include confrontational language in the title section of *Two-Headed Poems* only confirms her tie to the early Kristevan concept of poetic language.

Further describing the bourgeois North American audience and what it represses, Atwood continues:

> [O]n the whole, audiences prefer that art be not a mirror held up to life but a Disneyland of the soul, containing Romanceland, Spyland, Pornoland, and all the other Escapelands which are so much more agreeable than the complex truth. ... We are good at analyzing an author's production in terms of her craft. We are not good at analyzing it in terms of her politics, and by and large we do not do so.

> Our methods, in Canada, of controlling artists are not violent, but they do exist. We control through the marketplace and through critical opinion.

But despite those conditions, Atwood states, "[t]he writer, unless he is a mere word-processor, retains three attributes that power-mad regimes cannot tolerate; a human imagination ...; the power to communicate; and hope."[14] "Politics," the "marketplace," "imagination," and "hope" certainly interweave in *Two-Headed Poems*. An American marketplace in which socialist policies would be condemned as practices of unfair government subsidizing oppose socialist-feminist Canadians' imagination and hope. Her politics here address the relative powers of the two economies.

Criticism of *Two-Headed Poems* notes that it represents a change in Atwood's writing; I suggest that Atwood's poetic language emerges by an interconnecting of newly articulated political issues with a more direct voice. Typically, critical response to this work emphasizes its explicit feminism, its revived celebration of nature, or a joining of feminism and celebrations of nature.[15] Other readings see the change that this text represents in Atwood's work as tonal rather than thematic, a change toward compassion, hope, and realism.[16] One recent study argues that the two levels of language demand a psychological/psychoanalytic interpretation.[17] Showing Atwood's clearest commitment to Canadian socialist-feminism, *Two-Headed Poems* is, moreover, distinctive thematically and tonally, for its argument against the Americanization of Canada and for the statement of a cooperative ethic that Canadian women's history might provide.

To underscore the significance of this text, I suggest that it maps for Canadian women a promising narcissism according to the procedures that Luce Irigaray specifies. In Irigarayan terms, in this volume women become for one another in effective ways "[l]iving mirrors." Irigaray writes of a feminist specularization between mother and daughter:

> I came out of you, and here, in front of your very eyes, I am another living you.
>
> But, always distracted, you turn away. Furtively, you verify your own continued existence in the mirror, and you return to your cooking. ... I would like to ... let me watch you. And look at me. I would like us to play together at being the same and different. You/I exchanging selves endlessly and each staying herself. Living mirrors.
>
> We could play catch, you and I. But who would see that what bounces between us are images? That you give them to me, and I to you without end.[18]

In a process uncannily similar to that Irigaray describes, Atwood's speaker addresses her maternal forebears and discovers how they are both like and unlike her, how changing political conditions not only enable but further, in Atwood's view, demand that the speaker claim a public influence her mothers never dared precisely by drawing into the public sphere the mother's legacy to her. As Kristeva confirms in *Tales of Love*, such identification with another inheres in language, is expressed through language, and is further a form of love: "When the object that I incorporate is the speech of the other ... I bind myself to him [sic; masculine pronoun appears in the original French version as well] in a primary fusion, communion, unification. An identification" which is love.[19]

MORE MIRRORS

Mirrors appear in the poems encoding a progressive narcissism as well as in those that provide the volume's counterpoint, a masculinist imperialist order. In the eleven-poem title section, a Canadian speaker of unspecified gender addresses the United States directly, and in the shorter prose poem "Marrying the Hangman" a female narrator comments obliquely on Canadian-US relations by describing her crucial alliance with a Canadian man. The image of the mirror appears both in the anti-imperialist poems and in poems to women, so that regressive and progressive narcissism conflict sharply at the levels of theme and of rhetorical figuring. That figuring, combined with the confrontational language used for the first time in Atwood's work, set this volume apart as especially pertinent to a reading informed by Kristevan semiotics, her theory that subversive writing recalls a maternal order prior to the ordinary world of men, power politics, and conventional language.

The title of this volume and title sequence themselves figure Canada's difficult situation, its "two heads." Within the country, Trudeau "has two voices,"[20] referring in this case not to his bilingual fluency but to his duplicity in French-English Canadian relations and in Canada's relations with the United States. Under Trudeau's pro-American policies, Canada becomes America's "second head" (69). And, the speaker sees: "now everything / in the place is falling south" (59), but no matter, s/he continues, because "the family business / ... was too small anyway" (60). While the politicized speaker concedes the fiscal advantages of alliance with the United States, s/he still tries to imagine and defend Canadian alternatives; a Canadian faith in poetic language, in a speech that would bolster Canadian socialism and protect women as those most vulnerable to an open marketplace, struggles with an American economic pragmatism in the sequence.

The speaker is perhaps deliberately not gendered in order to champion the alliance between Canadian women and men and US feminists that Atwood prefers and opposes to a dangerous accord between Canadian and American men. The speaker describes the vocabulary of American capitalism as follows: "We see this language always / and merely as a disease / of the mouth. Also / as the hospital that will cure us, / distasteful but necessary" (73) — "cure us" of financial vulnerability while, on the other hand, the speaker muses in the same poem, "[s]urely in your language / no one can sing. ... // That is a language for ordering / the slaughter and gutting of hogs, for / counting stacks of cans. Groceries / are all you are good for. Leave / the soul to us. Eat shit" (73). This vulgar speech is new to Atwood's poetry, and its purpose is to defend an order some of whose central structuring principles defy economic pragmatism, an order sketched in by this and one other reference in the volume to the more impractical powers of those who "sing" and dream instead of "counting cans."

The speaker's attention to language as the ground of identity links *Two-Headed Poems* thematically with much of Atwood's other writing. The plain style of these poems, while not imaginative in any typical way on the surface, paradoxically defends a state in which the imaginative alternative a socialist ideal demands can survive.

"Our dreams ... / are of freedom" (74), the Canadian persona claims in the sequence's closing lines, having just described Canadians as those who "refuse / to believe the secrets of our hearts, /. . . moral as fortune cookies" (72). "Our hearts are virtuous, they swell / like stomachs at a wedding, / plump with goodwill" (72). But dreams and dream logic are inconsequential if they cannot at least be articulated, and they cannot be articulated as long as "[o]ur flag" is "silence" (63). "To save this [Canadian poetic] language," the persona asserts, "we needed echoes, / we needed to push back / the other words, the coarse ones / spreading themselves everywhere / like thighs or starlings" (64). We, Canadians, suffer from "atrophy of the tongue / the empty mirror" (60) while "[t]hose south of us are lavish / with their syllables. They scatter, we / hoard" (61). An "empty mirror" always calls up the therapeutically narcissistic process in Atwood's work.

The persona at its most exasperated then states the Canadian problem incisively, starting with the question, "whose language / is this anyway?":

You [Trudeau] want the air
but not the words that come with it:
breathe at your peril.

These words are yours,
though you never said them,
you never heard them, history
breeds death but if you kill
it you kill yourself.

What is a traitor?

This dense passage contains Atwood's doleful understanding of the process and effects of the Americanization of Canada: with economic identification comes an ideological overpowering by which America's history becomes Canada's. To fight that encroachment would label a Canadian as a traitor in the Canada of 1978, apparently, although the American definition of that term suggests precisely the rebelliousness that first distinguished American from Canadian history. The term "traitor" is differently defined by the two cultures, leaving the speaker caught between meanings. S/he clarifies that to understand its Canadian signification, Canadians must accept "the empty mirror" — silence in Atwood's writing — and discover in Canadian history by whom the term has been used, under what conditions, and to what ends.

This speaker surely views her/himself as a traitor to America, as a Canadian nationalist; an understanding of how Canadian left-nationalism has been and can be reproduced in one's own family becomes clearer beyond the text's title sequence, when the speaker becomes gendered female. Although the American persona in the title sequence refers to the subordinate culture in patronizing terms as "one / big happy family" (62), the place of the family in this and Atwood's other writings is in fact named as the site where change can begin to occur. If Trudeau is the leader or cultural father in this text, he is mirrored by the speaker's own mate, the father of her child, with whom, she laments in "Solstice Poem," she speaks "[w]orn language."

In part five of "Solstice Poem," the young mother speaking clarifies the two broad, structuring principles on which the text rests, the principle of aggression and the principle of human celebration:

> In this house
> ...
> my daughter dances
> unsteadily with a knitted bear.
>
> Her father, onetime soldier,
> touches my arm.
> Worn language clots our throats,
> making it difficult to say
> what we mean, making it
> difficult to see.
>
> Instead we sing in the back room, raising
> our pagan altar
> of oranges and silver flowers:
> our fools' picnic, our signal,
> our flame, our nest, our fragile golden
> protest against murder. (84)

In the fourth part of "Solstice Poem" the speaker initiates progressive narcissism, as "fragile" and difficult as it is, with the question, "How can I teach her [their daughter] / some way of being human / that won't destroy her?" (83), a question the speaker/mother seems uncertain she can answer:

> I would like to tell her, Love
> is enough
> ...
> Instead I will say in
> my crone's voice, Be
> ruthless when you have to, tell
> the truth when you can,
> when you can see it.
>
> Iron talismans, and ugly, but
> more loyal than mirrors. (83)

And she tries to find a "truth" she admits is hard to "see."

The speaker begins to extend her understanding of Canadian

women's pasts, the vulnerability they withstood by means of their friendships and common work, in the fourth of "Five Poems for Grandmothers" when she declares of the writing she undertakes that "against the small fears / of the very old, the fear / of mumbling, the fear of dying, / the fear of falling downstairs, / I make this charm / from nothing but paper; which is good," she adds, "for exactly nothing" (40). Still she makes the charm, and she does so significantly in a poem that traces her family lineage along maternal lines. In the third poem of the sequence she muses:

> Sons branch out, but
> one woman leads to another.
> Finally I know you [grandmother]
> through your daughters,
> my mother, her sisters,
> and through myself:
>
> Is this you, this edgy joke
> I make, are these your long fingers,
> your hair of an untidy bird,
> is this your outraged
> eye, this grip
> that will not give up?

A tenacity and "outrage[]" associated with a character such as Joan Foster's mother in *Lady Oracle* is here, finally, given meaningful voice in Atwood's work.

Other poems address the speaker's daughter and sister, poems whose tone, although still impassioned, contrasts distinctly with the hard rationalism of the text's critiques of international power politics. In "A Red Shirt" — an outstanding example — the speaker again brings female history to the foreground as two women together sew clothing for a child:

> The shirt we make is stained
> with our words, our stories.
>
> The shadows the light casts
> on the wall behind us multiply:

> This is the procession
> of old leathery mothers,
>
> ...
>
> mothers like worn gloves
> wrinkled to the shapes of their lives,
>
> passing the work from hand to hand,
> mother to daughter,
>
> a long thread of red blood, not yet broken.
> (102)

Women's work, a communal economy, not only provides an alternative to American capitalism but also underlines an ideological option, the "echoes" of the Canadian language referred to in the title sequence. "It may not be true," the speaker concedes in "A Red Shirt,"

> that one myth cancels another.
> Nevertheless, in a corner
> of the hem, where it will not be seen,
> where you will inherit
> it, I make this tiny
> stitch, my private magic. (104)

The history of Canada as described in *Two-Headed Poems* is metaphorically tied to nature and natural process, as in "BLACK STONE MOTHER GOD," for example, where the speaker's icon is chosen because "A river shaped her, / smoothed her with sand and battered / her against the shore, and she / resisted, she is still here" (89). In this poem the speaker adds the resonant powers of resistance her icon stands for to the greater process of progressive narcissism the text as a whole encodes. Resistance is made possible only after you recognize and "[w]orship what / you like, what you want / to be like. Old mother, / I pray to what is / and what refuses" (89). The two sisters sewing the shirt also acknowledge "the constant pull // of the earth's gravity furrowing / our bodies, tugging us down" (102).

By acknowledging that one thing Canadians share is nature, the speaker implies, they might awaken to a common language: "We do not walk on the earth / but in it," she claims, "all waves are one / wave; there is no other" (96). And in the closing lines of "All Bread" the speaker's vision of an alternative ethic finds its language in a loose but effective logic relating Canada's vast, impressive, and coveted natural endowment with its politics:

> Lift these ashes
> into your mouth, your blood;
> to know what you devour
> is to consecrate it,
> almost. All bread must be broken
> so it can be shared. Together
> we eat this earth. (108)

As humble a meal as "this earth" may supply, it seems preferable to the diet of "shit" s/he prescribes elsewhere.

"CANADIAN" LANGUAGE?

Canada overall shares with its undistinguished women a history of economic vulnerability, but a history also more communal. The claim that "powerless" Canadian women represent a subversive ethic becomes the premise of this volume's poetic language. What is problematic about the argument of *Two-Headed Poems*, of course, is that its speaker asks readers to place ultimate faith in the power to find in Canadian history, or more specifically in the history of its typical women, codes that will guard against the American marketplace. The world that occasions the poems, however, witnesses that "power" and "faith" are still irreducible opposites and that, indeed, even the speaker's language must refer to codes dominated by the American marketplace in order to be heard. This will be an unresolved question in Atwood's writing: whether Canadian language is now so strictly bound to the conditions of American production that it cannot be said to exist at all.

The "private magic" Atwood's young mother wills to her child may be no more effective in preventing erasure of Canadian socialist policies than "magic" is generally considered to be, but what seems most significant in these poems is that Atwood not only argues for disruptive speech but also shows how it is imagined and at what cost. In that way she earns the title "Canadian" on her own terms, and "poet" in Kristevan usage.[21] Thus her language becomes courageous and subversive, for she has published with a major North American publisher a volume that is openly and intelligently critical of a capitalist world order, encoding a socialist-feminist ethic unapologetically.

Near the middle of this volume comes a poem that has received little attention from critics, perhaps because it seems anomalous in this direct, passionate text. However, "Marrying the Hangman" is important because it reflects subtly the concerns and strategies informing the volume overall. Like Atwood's *The Journals of Susanna Moodie*, this much shorter piece renders imaginatively the real experience of a Canadian woman, in this case Françoise Laurent, who, Atwood's notes printed at the end of the volume explain, convinced the man in the cell next to hers to marry her and thus win their release from prison, also saving her life. He was imprisoned for duelling in 1751, she for stealing. "Except for letters of pardon," Atwood writes, "the only way at the time for someone under sentence of death to escape hanging was, for a man, to become the hangman, or, for a woman, to marry one" (111).

As in the title sequence, freedom is the issue here, and it comes according to the same process and with the same results: looking beyond the ruling order to find the one way out, a speaker in a highly vulnerable position refuses to accept the identity of the doomed and talks her way to safety. If the United States controls the North American media and in general holds greater power than Canada, it can be seen to occupy the same position structurally as the prison guards and legal system in this poem in an analogy which is, again, remarkable for its boldness in late-capitalist North America; the French-Canadian woman becomes all Canadian women in making contact with another in submissive conditions, agreeing to form the only bond that the system rewards. They are "freed" in this historical allegory, but the man's new occupation offers him no greater power than he had before imprisonment — he was "a drummer in the colonial troops at Quebec" (111) — and is, as well, probably not an occupation he would have chosen in normal circumstances.

Laurent, a servant condemned to death for stealing clothes from the wife of her employer (50), is in the end bound to a man she has never seen in the constraints of an eighteenth-century marriage. The poem's narrator asks, "What did she say when she discovered that she had left one locked room for another? They talked of love, naturally, though that did not keep them busy forever" (52). The poem ends, "He said: foot, boot, order, city, fist, roads, time, knife, // She said: water, night, willow, rope hair, earth belly, cave, meat, shroud, open, blood. // They both kept their promises" (52).

It seems possible that Atwood views the couple as mirrors of contemporary Canadian men and women in their relations with the United States. Canadian women hold an ideological position at the greatest possible remove from controlling American men; Canadian women convincing Canadian men to form allegiances with them rather than with American men results in the same positioning as in "Marrying the Hangman," and for the same reasons: American men remain in power in North America and yet the less powerful Canadians have at least survived. Canadian men still "work for" American men, but also Canadian women are still protected as that group who might be able somehow, through will and ingenuity, to preserve Canadianness. In Atwood's vocabulary, that is what values difference from a capitalist-imperialist ruling order and is essential as Canadian women gain public authority.

Canada's future in the shadow of the United States seems inevitable, but Canada has managed so far to maintain important differences, and it can continue to do so if empowered Canadians look not to masculinist Americans but to one another. The reality of American encroachment is balanced in *Two-Headed Poems* by reference to the powers of imagination, that which thinks beyond the codes of the ruling order, and Atwood's central personae defend the powers of poetic language again and again throughout the text. The most succinct expression of the process by which poetic language erupts comes in "Marrying the Hangman" when the fated servant plans her strategy:

To live in prison is to live without mirrors. To live without mirrors is to live without the self. She is living selflessly, she finds a hole in the stone wall and on the other side of the wall, a voice. The voice comes through darkness and has no face. This voice becomes her mirror. (49)

But the distinction between regressive and progressive, masculinist and feminist narcissism, usually following gender lines in Atwood's previous work, begins to appear as an internal split in her central female characters. Men no longer need propagate regressive narcissism (although with few exceptions they will do so in her latest work) because the existing power structures themselves do so, those that her women enter in the texts of the 1980s and 90s. American feminism becomes a thing quite apart from, and then again allied with, socialist feminist historiography in Canada in Atwood's next two novels, *Bodily Harm* and *The Handmaid's Tale*.

Chapter Four

POWER REVISITED: THE 1980s' TEXTS

ATWOOD'S WRITING in the late 1980s complicates the optimism of her work appearing in the mirror stage. Like the persona in *True Stories*, her poems published in 1981, Rennie Wilford in the novel *Bodily Harm* (1982) discovers in a dramatic moment that Canadian women's power of compassion on its own in a world dominated by narcissistic men amounts to little power at all. Feminist efficacy in Atwood's more recent work would apparently demand connection with thinking men whose relationships to existing structures remain as actively scrutinizing, if not indeed subversive, as that of a leftist feminist.

When Rennie is sent from the Caribbean island of St. Antoine, where she has become entangled in brutal politics, back to Toronto at novel's end, it is presumably to begin the final stage of progressive narcissism: the forming of alliances that weld the subversive identities and speech of Atwood's earlier women to Canada's most promising male-invented political structures in order to produce newly radicalized subjects, both women and men. In other words, it is left to Rennie and Atwood's other female speakers in the 1980s' texts to attempt to redefine power by joining "male" socialist political philosophy with experiences of love and work between women.

Whereas the defensive kind of power wielded by young men fearful of disintegration of the social order they inherit has always been seen as harmful in Atwood's texts, another kind, held by men in marginal positions like her women, has quietly persisted. The project of Atwood's characters in this period seems to be active critique, undertaken by Canadian women and the men they choose, of the same structures her unsympathetic male characters pathetically work to uphold. What, then, ought to remain to the scrutinizing, favourable characters in the later texts are structures enabling a social-ist-feminist order. But Atwood's most successful novel to date, *The Handmaid's Tale* (1985), a dystopia set in the United States in approximately the year 2010, represents the opposite order: a totali-tarian state ruled by fundamentalist Christian men determined at any cost to make America potent again. In the pair of texts studied in this chapter — *Bodily Harm* and *The Handmaid's Tale* — the first does not demand or enable the second but instead calls for its reverse.

Serious economic problems are among the many overwhelming global crises that are said in *The Handmaid's Tale* to have brought on the Republic of Gilead. That same economic crisis has already been prepared for in Atwood's work in the valuing of a feminist socialism. And "I'm defining my feminism," she said in a 1983 interview, "as human equality and freedom of choice."[1] In Atwood's view, feminist socialism professes the best of North American economic thought, "human equality," at the same time as it promotes the "freedom of choice" associated with the contemporary women's movement.

BODILY HARM

In this novel, it is necessary for the protagonist, Rennie Wilford, to enter a milieu in every way remote from Toronto and her more rural Ontario girlhood before she can begin to perceive at all clearly the potential value of her Canadian home. Critical studies of *Bodily Harm* begin to combine questions of feminism, nationalism, and the efficacy of language, and they avoid centring on the novel's genre, generic studies of Atwood's work overall having decreased remarkably in the 1980s.[2] Most studies focus the issues of feminism, nationalism, and language in the characterization of Rennie. While some deny Rennie positive change and read the novel as a failure in that way,[3] the majority of opinion (including mine) affirms her or her author's politicization.[4]

As the force that threatens to obliterate the Canadian difference, regressive narcissism appears now most menacingly not only in American or Canadian men but rather in the Canadian woman, Rennie, whose mirror stage is the most prolonged and dangerous but also potentially the most effective of those experienced by Atwood's central females. The lack in this text, however, appears in the absence of a more or less sympathetic Canadian male, like Duncan, Joe, Chuck Brewer (the Canadian poet in *Lady Oracle*), or the male aspect of the ungendered speaker in *Two-Headed Poems*, a man also effectively linked to the protagonist and to existing political structures. Daniel, Rennie's surgeon and lover, begins to fill the place of the sympathetic male but, because he is happily married, ends his affair with Rennie; as a medical doctor tending to the private rather than the public sphere his realm of influence is in any case limited. By now in Atwood's texts this absence of a working connection between women and men seems ominous, and it is emphasized by the appearance on the novel's closing pages of two indifferent Canadian men, one of whom in particular, the government official who rescues Rennie, suggests in his euphemistic detachment from the political situation around him that hope for the future of Canadian socialist feminism is slim indeed. As Atwood's women in the recent texts have acceded to and been corrupted by regressive narcissism, they have also finally retrieved their potential for renewing change in vividly drawn mirror stages. Her promising Canadian men in these texts, however, have failed to become effective.

The islands where this text is set have recently emerged from British rule and are "renaming everything"[5] but are also suffering under the CIA-controlled leader who murders his rivals regularly and without reprisal. Meanwhile, financial and material aid flows to the dangerously corrupt leadership from an unsuspecting and uninvolved Canadian government. By implication, this Canadian government, run of course largely by men, becomes what Rennie must ally herself with, first to escape the islands and then to supplement the power she earns through her Caribbean experiences, yet from the beginning that government is clearly made to seem ridiculous in its disengaged, undiscriminating benevolence.

On an assignment-holiday to write up the islands she visits in a light travel piece for potential tourists, Rennie, another product of bourgeois, small-town Ontario, like Marian McAlpin of *The Edible Woman*, is primarily attempting to recover from breast cancer, a partial mastectomy, and the resulting abandonment by her mate. Unlike Marian, however, Rennie starts her movement toward self-knowledge in that state of disorientation beyond or behind mirrors. Always initiating progressive narcissism in Atwood's work, this state appears at the beginning of the novel rather than near the end, as in the previous three: when Rennie feels that on the Caribbean island of St. Antoine "she's invisible ... safe," (39) appropriately in her hotel room the "mirror over the bureau is small" (48). From the first, Rennie is forced by her lack of familiar mirrorings and the language and behaviour that attend them to reconstruct an identity not from North American media images but from the people around her.

Rennie clearly fails at first to represent the fully politicized speaker that Atwood's texts have led to, but neither is she caught irremediably in regressive narcissism as embodied by Atwood's males, represented here by the domineering and emotionally facile Jake, Rennie's Toronto lover. Jake, in a manner similar to that of his predecessors in Atwood's work, especially Peter and David, views his female lover as "one of the things [he] was packaging" (104); he "liked thinking of sex as something he could win at" (207). Jake leaves Rennie because "[h]e could not bear to see her vulnerable" (201) with breast cancer. But Jake receives little emphasis in the narrative, leaving Rennie to recover and define herself alone in relation to the men and women she meets amid the violent political upheaval on St. Antoine.

Early in the text Rennie's late transformation is signalled by a character sketch that links her to her small-town Ontario past, her female lineage, and the experience of progressive narcissism she will undergo. "Once she had ambitions," she muses, "which she now thinks of as illusions. ... Then she graduated and it was no longer 1970.

Several editors pointed out to her that she could write what she liked, there was no law against it, but no one was under any obligation to pay her for doing it, either" (63-64):

> Now that she no longer suffers from illusions, Rennie views her kind of honesty less as a virtue than a perversion, one from which she still suffers, true; ... like ... those other diseases typical of Griswold [Ontario] ... a professional liability. (64)

> The other problem is the reputation she's getting for being too picky. ... [I]ncreasingly there are things she can't seem to do. Maybe it isn't *can't*, maybe it's *won't*. What she wants is something legitimate to say. (65-66)

Her "honesty" is from the start tied to her family history in Griswold, a history populated almost exclusively by women in Rennie's memory; her aunts, her mother, her grandmother. And an integrity matched with recovered human feeling will produce the Rennie capable of "something legitimate to say" very late in this text.

As if to point toward the dismantling of the binary pair male/female, a dismantling which Atwood envisions as a result of progressive narcissism, Rennie is here directly guided toward Canadian feminist consciousness by a man, the apparently uncorrupted Caribbean politician Dr. Minnow, who begins by teaching her that "[e]veryone is in politics here, my friend ... all the time. Not like the sweet Canadians" (124). Minnow deliberately monitors Rennie's stay on St. Antoine and insists that she be aware of all of the effects of Canadian aid there. Early on he notes as the two fly toward the island that "'[w]hen we had our hurricane, the sweet Canadians donated a thousand tins of ham, Maple Leaf Premium. It was for the refugees.' He laughs, as if this is a joke, but Rennie doesn't get it. 'The refugees never see this ham,' he says, explaining patiently" (29). In this same scene Minnow repeats the epithet "sweet Canadians," those people who "are famous for their good will" (29), an epithet the American drug-trafficker, gun-runner, and briefly Rennie's lover, Paul, corroborates by calling Rennie "nice" and "naive" (150, 245). Paul tries to explain that "[s]he's led a sheltered life" (147) and indeed successfully draws her into the island's treacheries almost without her knowledge or consent. Paul takes the place of the ever-present narcissistic lover of Atwood's protagonists, and his American nationality only further stresses the dangerous, critical absence of a promising and effective Canadianized male figure in this text.

While Minnow's place in the novel argues for a deconstructed reading of gender, such speculation about sexual politics would, unfortunately, elude Rennie, whose primary concerns as a features writer until the novel's two opening events (her recounting her surgery and near encounter with a rapist/murderer) had been Toronto "trends" (25) and "[s]urfaces" (26), avoiding what is in "bad taste" (26-27) or "out of date" (135). Minnow as guide to Rennie's culminating feminist experiences, because he is a man, problematizes her final assertion that "she's afraid of men because men are frightening" (290). All strategies Rennie clings to in order to remain within "the effect she aims for, neutrality ... [i]nvisibility" (15) in fact fall away in the extreme climactic circumstances of imprisonment with another woman in a tiny cell.

A debased idea of feminism not as a force for social change but as a process by which women somehow become like men, it is important to note, seems "out of date" to Rennie who, even after the intruder breaks into her apartment and leaves behind his murder weapon, "didn't want to turn into the sort of woman who was afraid of men" (40) and who explicitly "did not feel in need of support" (163) from other women. Rennie has felt contempt for such feminism while her real, profound need for identification with other women has been silenced and repressed. Her closest friend, reminiscent of such dubious female confidantes as Ainsley in *The Edible Woman*, Anna in *Surfacing*, and Marlene in *Lady Oracle*, is the punk clothing store owner Jocasta, with whom Rennie has a connection no more intimate or sustaining than previous protagonists have had with their earlier counterparts. Although Rennie's transformation will occur precisely because of her finally accepting connection with one of these pathetic women, Lora — another Ontarian, living on St. Antoine and as hopelessly vulnerable to men as her predecessors in

Atwood's texts — Lora disappears in the narrative, and Rennie will return to Toronto alone.

It is Dr. Minnow's predictions that touch directly upon Rennie's therapeutic journey back to Canada and indirectly upon her return to connection with other women. Urging her to "[l]ook with your eyes open ... since you are a reporter, it is your duty" (134), Minnow also implicitly calls her to "[t]he love of your own country" (133) although such love is a "terrible curse," he admits, because it incites you to try to "change things" (133). In his campaign speech Minnow specifies his reasons for entering politics in language closest of any in Atwood's fiction to her own opinions as stated in her critical prose: Minnow fights the CIA-ruled incumbent, he explains to Rennie, "because everyone tells you it is not possible. They cannot imagine things being different. It is my duty to imagine, and they know that for even one person to imagine is very dangerous to them, my friend" (229). Minnow, who is assassinated by the incumbent Prime Minister Ellis, indirectly asks Rennie to "imagine things being different" between St. Antoine and a comparatively wealthy and powerful country such as Canada, it seems, so that Canada's "good will" can become more effective. By propelling Rennie to reconsider the value of her home, he indirectly sends her back to Griswold, Ontario, and the community of women from which Rennie has tried to escape.

Rennie is in some ways already prepared for the feminist historiography that comprises the middle part of successful progressive narcissism by her surgery for cancer, after which she could no longer believe "she was unique" (23). Also, her refusal to write the feature article on "pornography as an art form" (211) for a fashionable Toronto magazine hints at her felt need for identification with women as a starting point for identification with others. And her experience with the male intruder and then with male police officers further alert her to a menacing sexism which, like anything else that forces her beneath "surfaces," she prefers to ignore. But before Rennie can reclaim her female past, she must first pursue many painful and intricately connected memories of women, which she does as her safety on St. Antoine diminishes.

Having seen the lives of women when growing up in small-town Ontario as tedious and constrained, Rennie tries to escape, believing that "I didn't want to be trapped, like my mother. Although I admired her — ... she was practically a saint — I didn't want to be like her in any way, I didn't want to ... be anyone's mother, ever" (58). She also acknowledges, however, that "it's not always so easy to get rid of Griswold" (18).

In the course of the novel Rennie in fact returns to and reclaims her past, accepting her mother's "saintliness" but transforming and galvanizing it in order to move it beyond Griswold into a more public sphere. Like Canada itself in this novel, Rennie's mother, recalling the parents in *Surfacing* with their "perilous innocence" and the sweet-tempered Aunt Lou in *Lady Oracle*, seems blameless but ineffective, and in order to find the renewed identity Rennie comes to believe she needs she must choose to empower the goodness which both her matrilineage and national history provide by joining it to subversive writing.

Very shortly before Rennie must revive a badly beaten Lora in their shared cell, she dreams of her grandmother in Griswold and therefore her female heritage, as though to signal the first result of progressive narcissism, finding an effective voice. Holding Lora and calling her name, Rennie acknowledges that her healing speech "is a gift" (299), and then Lora begins to regain consciousness. The gift of healing is further tied in this novel to women's enduring, unspoken powers in the character of Elva, the Caribbean grandmother and masseuse who informs Rennie that the "magic" (194) of her hands, too, is "a gift, I have it from my grandmother. ... [S]he pass it to me" (193). And women's magic has appeared most obviously before when the speaker in *Two-Headed Poems* is sewing for her daughter, as well as in the reunions with their mothers of Joan in *Lady Oracle* and the narrator in *Surfacing*.

Having revived Lora, Rennie changes from a woman who, through fear, "can't make a sound" (293) in protest as Lora is beaten, to one whose resolve is to become a "reporter. She will pick her time, then she will report" (301), if she survives. The "way she sees" (300) has been dramatically altered, especially, it seems, the way she sees herself and her past. Although Atwood's readers may feel disappointed at Rennie's entrapment in the future tense — "she *will* report" (my emphasis) — we may also identify positively with her change of will.

The experiences late in the novel show that what Rennie had lost by renouncing her mother was specifically her ability to feel empathy. She explains earlier that she refuses to be "*in love*" because "[i]t made you visible, soft, penetrable; it made you ludicrous":

> It was foolhardy, and if you got through it without damage it was only by sheer luck. It was like taking off your clothes at lunchtime in a bank. It let people think they knew something about you that you didn't know about them, it gave them power over you. (102)

Rennie "wants to remember someone she's loved, she wants to remember loving someone. It's hard to do" (283), and in their cell, when Lora cries, Rennie thinks she should offer "comfort" and "[c]ompassion," that "[s]he ought to go over to Lora and put her arms around her and pat her on the back, but she can't" (288). In that way Rennie has been affected by regressive narcissism, one sign of which is repression of feeling associated with intimacy, vulnerability, interconnection. And yet her increasing sensitivity beginning early in the novel hints that she will be able to undergo the process of progressive narcissism which, among its other effects, restores emotion, joining power and love.

And the "luck" which she notes must accompany love in order for love to endure is the same luck offered her by the recurring homeless figure who shakes Rennie's hand (75), a quality associated, too, with Dr. Minnow's imaginative "[f]aith" (227) in change and with Elva's magic. Most importantly, luck, the power that enables Rennie to feel empathy, attends her in the novel's closing sentences when "[s]he will never be rescued. She has already been rescued. She is not exempt. Instead she is lucky, suddenly, finally, she's overflowing with luck, it's this luck holding her up" (301). Again, as in *Two-Headed Poems*, Atwood calls a central character to risk an imaginative leap, trusting that belief in positive change allows for change. Belief equals faith equals luck, conditions enabling a preferable social order and standing in direct opposition to the suspicious and embittered states of mind of Atwood's pathological characters.

MIRRORS IN THE 1980S

Such pathological characters are, not surprisingly, associated with mirror imagery that appears rarely but strategically. At the Barbados airport *en route* to St. Antoine Rennie "examines her face in the mirror, checking for signs. ... [S]he looks normal ... [not] peculiar" (15). Forced on the island to manage without this safe and bland self-image, Rennie is repeatedly confronted with the phenomenon of mirrored sunglasses worn by the corrupt politicians and by her American lover Paul, a man whose faith in reforming change has left him. As long as Rennie allows herself to see herself only as reflected in the artificial gaze of such men, she will not choose subversive language but rather will believe, as Paul claims, that "[t]here's only people with power and people without power. Sometimes they change places, that's all" (240) and that "democracy and fair play and all those ideas" are "shit" (247). Rennie seems in the end headed for the more Canadian position from which power itself can be redefined and redistributed, moving away from what she finally recognizes as Paul's need for maintaining the status quo, a state allowing violence. "He loves it, thinks Rennie. That's why we get into these messes: because they love it" (256). Choosing to love compassion instead, Rennie turns from regressive narcissism in its most sinister, destructive form, represented by the characters of the Caribbean male politicians other than Minnow, toward the Canadian Lora, with whom indeed she thought throughout the novel she had "nothing in common" (271), and to their shared heritages.

Rennie seems to be rescued, although whether or not she hallucinates her release from prison is left unclear, and she then meets "the gentleman from the Canadian government" (293) who is wearing "tinted glasses and ... [a] safari jacket" (294). To the dazed, filthy, and malnourished Rennie he offers an expensively packaged cigarette and "[h]e smiles at her, he's a little nervous. He says she certainly has given them some uneasy moments" (294), and he continues:

> The government can't make a public apology of course but they would like her to know unofficially that they consider it a regrettable incident. They understand that she is a journalist and such things should not happen to journalists. It was an error. They hope she's prepared to consider it in the same light.
>
> To tell you the truth ... they thought you were an agent. Of a foreign government. A subversive. Isn't that absurd? ... [H]e's leading up to something, here it comes. He says he realizes she's a journalist but in this instance things are very delicate. ... (294-295)

Rennie finally responds, "I suppose you're telling me not to write about what happened to me," and he answers, "Requesting. ... Of course we believe in freedom of the press. But for them it's a matter of saving face" (295). To finish this character off, Atwood lets him speak the doubts Rennie is perceiving, that as Canadians "we don't make value judgements ... we just allocate aid for peaceful development, but *entre nous* we wouldn't want another Grenada on our hands" (296).

As though this strategically placed representative of the Canadian government is not discouraging enough, Atwood has Rennie meet a Canadian man on her flight home, a man in the computer industry who teases her for not getting a better Caribbean tan. She realizes in their brief, terse conversation that "[s]he has no intention of telling the truth [to him], she knows she will not be believed. In any case she is a subversive. She was not one once but now she is" (300-301), whether or not her subversive consciousness can have any effect on the culture to which she returns.

THE HANDMAID'S TALE

By setting *The Handmaid's Tale* in the United States amid a milieu which seems to represent the effects of a regressive narcissism gone unimpeded, Atwood further punctuates Rennie's isolation in mid-1980s' Toronto. Rennie has in the past failed to find colleagues, lovers, and friends — that is, a community — with whom she can live less endangered by violent forms of power; Atwood implies that if North American women and men cannot or will not effectively meet current national and international crises, especially economic, then a state like that of the Republic of Gilead could conceivably result. Political scientist Charles Taylor describes in his *The Malaise of Modernity* the kind of tyranny that might result from the failure to form communities dedicated to change:

> A society in which people end up as the kind of individuals who are "enclosed in their own hearts" is one where few will want to participate actively in self-government. They will prefer to stay at home and enjoy the satisfactions of private life, as long as the government of the day produces the means to these satisfactions and distributes them widely. ... This opens the danger of a new, specifically modern form of despotism ... It will not be a tyranny of terror and oppression as in the old days. The government will be mild and paternalistic.[6]

But the government of the former United States in *The Handmaid's Tale* is violently repressive, aggressive, and male, the opposite, that is, of the tolerant feminist-socialist order Atwoodian narcissism aims for. Even in Gilead, however, Atwood's female protagonist undergoes the mirror stage in full, resulting in her literal liberation, to Canada, because she has reclaimed her mother and joined forces with other subversive, marginal characters. She has learned to speak her honest and therefore subversive language in the tape she makes on her escape north. But why is *The Handmaid's Tale* set in the United States? The majority of reviewers read this text as a critique of American feminism.[7] Amid the wealth of essay-length pieces respecting Atwood's most successful work, those which address its status as dystopian science fiction are most numerous.[8] Generic studies[9] and those that treat the politics of reading[10] or language[11] comprise another group. And, treatments of history[12] and historical materialism[13] are several.

While there is good reason to agree with the initial book reviewers who read the novel as critical of 1960s' and 1970s' American feminism, the novel can also be addressed as a critique, more specifically, of regressive narcissism as it has affected American feminists. The mother of Offred, the protagonist, is as invaluable finally as her predecessors in Atwood's work, the older generation of Ontario women. The qualities her daughter rejects about her become the very things necessary for Offred's (as for *Surfacing*'s narrator's and Joan's) survival. North American women will inevitably and fatally turn against one another, Atwood seems to warn, unless the loving connections between them are maintained and, optimally, joined to the powers of leftist North American men. Canadian women like Rennie in *Bodily Harm* ought to look to American women such as the subversives in *The Handmaid's Tale* (Ofglen, Moira), Atwood suggests, for that enabling alliance with which Canadian men usually fail to provide them. Such an obviously compromising, transnational, heterosexual feminism may seem indeed a shadowy version of Atwood's characters' politics in the 1970s, but it is feminism of a kind and it survives, as it does not in the official power structures of Gilead.

In this novel Atwood's contemptible minor female characters have been given power of the violent kind and appear as the tyrannical Aunts. A perhaps sympathetic, promising male lover has in fact married the protagonist but has also probably been killed; another subversive male becomes Offred's lover and seems responsible for her escape. Thus the gender of characters begins to matter less to Atwood in this text than their ability or inability to interrogate and undermine the governing order. Men can be "women," or leftist feminists; women can be "men," or sexist conservatives. Similarly, Canadians can be "Americans," Americans "Canadians," for this widely read novel with its American heroes undercuts many of Atwood's own working distinctions between Canada and the United States.

What matters consistently in Atwood's production is that which enables socialist feminism: women's attempting to associate themselves with their own history. Knowledge of that past will guard North American women against harmful pursuits of a kind of power not redefined in a system as yet unchanged. A dying system in

Atwood's view, it can be displaced by feminist socialism or, if women deny their historical and emotional bonds, with a system even more rigidly oppressive than what is in place now. Alliances with men who are not regressively narcissistic is necessary, too, but those alliances will not work until women acknowledge the valuable lessons of their common vulnerability and insist upon introducing acceptance and understanding of vulnerability into the public sphere. The resulting social order must, in other words, give value to human need in a dismantling of the pair of terms "power" and "love."

Like Atwood's other females, Offred undergoes a return to acceptance of her mother by way of mirroring experiences. Although early in the narrative Offred confides, in language close to that of other Atwood protagonists, that "I admired my mother in some ways, although things between us were never easy. She expected too much from me," [14] Offred comes to value for its freeing powers her mother's very "cockiness, her optimism and energy, her pizzazz" (265). In the process of redeeming her mother's legacy, Offred must learn to trust and form bonds with those who question the ruling order by seeing herself mirrored in those characters.

MIRRORS AGAIN

Significantly, the kind of mirror-gazing that indicates regressive narcissism in Atwood's work, always coded to the specular figure itself, pertains not only to the ruling men but to the memory of 1970s' and 1980s' feminists who acceded to unrevised forms of power. Male reaction to women who had exacerbated their pathology by refusing to value male potency, especially highly trained and independent professional women and lesbians, are imprisoned in a Gilead whorehouse where mirrors abound. Offred's Commander, head of the household where she is kept and part of the dominant regime but drawn to Offred beyond her role as host for his sperm, shows Offred an underground copy of *Vogue* from an earlier time. She stares at the photographs which,

> suggested an endless series of possibilities, extending like two

mirrors set facing one another, stretching on, replica after replica, to the vanishing point. They suggested one adventure after another, one wardrobe after another, one improvement after another, one man after another. They suggested rejuvenation, pain overcome and transcended, endless love. The real promise in them was immortality.

There they were again, the images of my childhood: bold, striding, confident, their arms flung out as if to claim space, their legs apart, feet planted squarely on the earth. ... Those candid eyes ... like the eyes of a cat, fixed for the pounce. ... Pirates, these women, with their ladylike briefcases for the loot and their horsy, acquisitive teeth. (165)

The "acquisitive" figures in the *Vogue* photos gain better definition through Offred's other recollections. In the novel's opening paragraph, for example, she explains that in former time a "yearning" pervaded; "we yearned for the future" (13) when all unfulfilled desire would be granted. Later she adds that "[i]t's strange to remember how we used to think, as if everything were available to us, as if there were no contingencies, no boundaries; as if we were free to shape and reshape forever the ever-expanding perimeter of our lives" (239) in psychological patterns clearly of the regressively narcissistic kind. A condition of progressive narcissism, on the other hand, insists upon acknowledgement of human limitation and interdependence, incorporates the past rather than longs for the future, and enables not ultimate individual efficacy and autonomy but rather communal identity and the limited powers of mutual trust.

Offred does achieve the movement to progressive narcissism precisely by trusting two politically engaged characters. Of her lover, Nick, whose underground connections probably free her, she acknowledges when they meet alone for the first time accidentally that "for the moment we're mirrors" (109), and concerning Ofglen, one of the text's female subversives, she observes "[s]he's like my own reflection, in a mirror" (54). Nick's last words to her as she escapes are simply "[t]rust me" (306), which Offred finally has done, learning in a moment of the muted optimism typical of Atwood's work that "[t]here can be alliances even in such places, even under such circumstances. This is something you can depend upon: there will always be alliances" (139).

Appropriately, when Offred has gotten away and pauses to make the tapes that tell her tale, she reflects not upon brutality or injustice or oppression but "forgiveness," in that tone of restored human compassion that always signals completion of the mirror stage and successful narcissistic experiences in Atwood's work. Offred continues:

> forgiveness ... is a power. To beg for it is a power, and to withhold or bestow it is a power, perhaps the greatest.
>
> Maybe none of this is about control. Maybe it isn't really about who can own whom, who can do what to whom and get away with it, even as far as death. ... Maybe it's about who can do what to whom and be forgiven for it. Never tell me it amounts to the same thing. (144-145)

While she does not specify who should be forgiven, she might refer at least in part to her mother and the activist legacy of contemporary American feminists, if she has come to accept the primary importance of women's history. For Atwood's women, forgetting their often quite unglamorous links to other women remains among the most dangerous patterns they can fall into. Although the American Offred achieves successful reconnections with her mother and with other women and forms an effectively radical affiliation with a man, surviving to tell her tale, the question of the status of Canadian women in *fin de siècle* North American culture remains unanswered.

❖

Chaper Five

WOMEN AND MEN
INTO THE 1990s

IN ATWOOD'S POETRY of the mid-1980s her persona, presumably a Canadian woman, assumes a voice perilously close to what might be a mature Rennie Wilford returned to the "glitzy" Toronto of the late 1970s, which Atwood has further described as "up to its eyeballs in narcissism."[1] A politicized subject in this dangerously unstable milieu — unstable because lacking in trusted leadership — the persona of *Interlunar* confesses that "I seem to myself to be without power. / To have the power of waiting merely. / Waiting to be told what to say. / But who will tell me?" Such a position describes various Atwoodian personae in her other writing of the late 1980s and early 1990s; *Cat's Eye* (1988), and *Wilderness Tips* (1991).

While Rennie's closing resolution to join integrity and action heralds politically engaged journalism, a kind of subversive speech, Atwood's works of poetry in the 1980s show speakers who are notably silent and apolitical. Having argued that politically engaged language results when Canadian women reclaim their histories and incorporate them at the level of public influence, Atwood's own poetic language takes neither new forms nor addresses new topics in the 1980s. *Interlunar* (1984) and the "New Poems 1985-1986" section of her *Selected Poems II* (1986) maintain familiar themes in a familiar idiom: gender power imbalances persist, and women's romantic fantasies fed by the media, including literature, support them. Relatedly, those power imbalances allow or encourage imbalances of other kinds, while the natural world, by contrast, provides a model of perfect balance. Hope is somehow still possible, however, through language imaginatively used.

"The Healer" and "The Saints" also people the 1984 volume *Interlunar*,[2] and, like all of the Canadian women before her in Atwood's novels who are outside the arenas of great influence, the healer states, "[t]he power is in me, but what for? / What am I to do with my hands in this tidy place / filled with those who do not want / to be truly healed?" (38). Yet this enduringly optimistic, stubbornly naive speaker continues that "I still / believe in free will" (85), admonishing an unspecified audience to "[t]ake your life in your hands" (85), "hardness of the heart can kill you" (86). Atwood perhaps addresses herself and her writer's task in these poems, hoping that she can tell herself "what to say" next. As Julia Kristeva explains simply in *Black Sun*, "those in despair are mystics" and as such beyond language; thus poetic language can give way to the absence of words.[3] And the milieu of Atwood's latest poetry seems to match exactly that of her 1988 novel, *Cat's Eye*.

CAT'S EYE

This novel[4] contains no socialist-Canadian males and no politically effective females. Elaine Risley, the successful artist whose recollections of a Toronto girlhood form the story, is like Rennie in *Bodily Harm* in that she feels quite in control of her career and her relations with men. Elaine is thus feminist in a popular sense of the term. More importantly, however, she is bewildered by her relations with other women — also like Rennie — until she reunites with the central figures in her youth: her mother, her friend Cordelia, and another friend's mother, Mrs. Smeath. Having existed for forty years only as unconscious and profoundly compelling subjects for her art, these women must enter Elaine's conscious memory in the novel's climactic moments. As always in Atwood's fiction, such moments reconnect the central character with her feelings, especially her emotional bond to other women.

Interpreters of *Cat's Eye* invariably comment upon the climactic
scene in which Elaine confronts and forgives Cordelia's treachery.[5]
Judith McCombs comments further, as I do, on Elaine's need to re-
establish ties with other female figures as well on her journey back.[6]
Generic studies of this novel have also appeared.[7] The hateful Mrs.
Smeath, for example, like Elizabeth's dreaded aunt in *Life Before Man*
and like Lora in *Bodily Harm*, represents what the main female figure
believes she defines herself in opposition to: woman as victimized and
victimizing. Elaine, by contrast, is successful and in control, but at
the expense of denying her connection with other women, especially
those most vulnerable. She will revise her views of Mrs. Smeath, and
of her own mother, in this novel's mirroring experiences.

Her reclamation of the figure who inspires a number of Elaine's
grotesquely appealing paintings happens quietly as Elaine views her
own work at a retrospective devoted to it. She pauses at a cluster of
pieces featuring Mrs. Smeath and realizes that

> I put a lot of work into that imagined body, white as a burdock
> root, flabby as pork-fat. Hairy as the inside of an ear. I laboured on
> it, with, I now see, considerable malice. But these pictures are not
> only mockery, not only desecration. ...
>
> It's the eyes I look at now. I used to think these were self-right-
> eous eyes, piggy and smug inside their wire frames; and they are.
> But they are also defeated eyes, uncertain and melancholy, heavy
> with unloved duty. The eyes of someone for whom God was a
> sadistic old man; the eyes of a small-town threadbare decency. Mrs.
> Smeath was a transplant to the city, from somewhere a lot smaller.
> A displaced person; as I was.
>
> Now I can see myself, through these painted eyes of Mrs.
> Smeath: a frazzle-headed ragamuffin from heaven knows where, a
> gypsy practically, with a heathen father and a feckless mother who
> traipsed around in slacks and gathered weeds. ... And yet she took
> me in.
>
> Some of this must be true. ...
>
> An eye for an eye leads only to more blindness. (404-405)

I will place considerable interpretive weight upon the simple clause "[a]nd yet she took me in," because it is the only instance in which Elaine acknowledges desirable connection with the older woman. Mrs. Smeath clearly stood in for Elaine's mother during the first year Elaine spent in Toronto, and her reclamation of the mother-imago — as well as the mother herself — is thus as necessary and profoundly moving as it always is in Atwood's fiction.

Elaine's mother does not fit the late 1940s' Toronto milieu, appearing "feckless" to the other women her age, "wild" (130) and "airy" (157) to the young Elaine. Significantly, too, Elaine perceives that her mother is "powerless" (157) against Elaine's girlhood tormentors. The world of public efficacy and self-assertion remains male and apart from the women's milieu so precisely rendered in this text; thus the feminism that finally emerges in its final moments remains at best a process of emotional and psychological healing. However valuable, such feminism lacks political force, as it does in Atwood's other realistic fiction of the late 1970s and the 1980s. Elaine sees that while "daytime is ruled by mothers ... [d]arkness brings home the fathers, with their real, unspeakable power" (157).

Although her mother has a kind of power, a kind which I argue Elaine adopts in her visit to Toronto as a middle-aged woman (and the kind which other Atwoodian heroines inherit from their mothers and mother-imagos), it never intersects with the "real, unspeakable power" of men in the public sphere. Such is the failed promise of current Canadian culture that Atwood's 1980s' fiction, poetry, and social criticism encode. But the move toward a progressive narcissism, with its particularly Atwoodian feminist turn, persists even here. Elaine reclaims not only her mother's heritage but also that of the two other dominant female figures from her youth in this novel's denouement, and Atwood calls attention to the process by placing it in the most strategic narrative position. Still, however, Elaine's journey is inward and solitary. Her renewed consciousness of shaping experiences from her childhood moves her because it results in reconnection with her feelings, opening her again to vulnerability and change at a time in her life when she is beginning to come to terms with these things.

She can more wisely enter her second half-century with the knowledge that her inward journey has provided, and yet she remains alone.

In the end Elaine seems quite like the influential women of the novel — her mother, Mrs. Smeath, Cordelia — just as Atwood's other fictional heroines all finally appear like their mothers, aunts, and youthful girlfriends. As Elaine's mother is dying, Elaine reveals that "I'm aware of a barrier between us. It's been there for a long time. Something I have resented. I want to put my arms around her. But I am held back" (397). Elaine's sense of her mother as powerless keeps Elaine from identifying too closely with her, and yet, unconsciously, Elaine has adopted her mother's strongest personality trait. As a teenager Elaine records that her mother "says she doesn't give a hoot" about how she dresses, for example, and Elaine muses that "*[n]ot giving a hoot* would be a luxury. It describes the fine, irreverent carelessness I myself would like to cultivate, in these and other matters" (214). Afraid to become like her mother and therefore to remain powerless, as she was at the hands of Cordelia, Elaine represses connection with her mother, only to act much as readers guess her mother might have acted at the Toronto retrospective devoted to her art. Having achieved success, Elaine need no longer fear disempowerment. She dresses in a jogging suit for her newspaper interview, and she answers with a candour and insouciance precisely like her mother's. Then, at the opening of her show, Elaine admits frankly that "I am swept with longing. I want my mother to be here" (351). Soon after that admission, Elaine begins to believe, for the first time since her youthful trauma, that perhaps another woman "really does like me" (411). One of the organizers of the retrospective tells Elaine that "[w]e're all very proud of you" (410), and Elaine perhaps begins to believe that.

Elaine's reclamation of her mother's influence is painless and unremarkable compared with her relations to Mrs. Smeath. The malicious, unfeeling aspect of Elaine's personality seems clearly linked to the figure of Mrs. Smeath, and it is this aspect that, ironically, enables Elaine to survive her young adulthood and indeed fosters her success as a painter. But its harmful effects are also shown in Elaine's judgmental treatment of her associate Susie, a young woman who becomes pregnant by the lover whom she and Elaine share, their art teacher, Josef. When Elaine answers Susie's desperate call and finds Susie near death as the result of a self-induced abortion, Elaine echoes thoughtlessly the words Mrs. Smeath once directed at her: "It serves her right" (321). Only when Elaine has fully accepted the legacies of the other two powerful figures from her youth, her mother and Cordelia, can she temper the harshness of her attitudes toward other women, attitudes learned through Mrs. Smeath's treatment of her.

Like Elaine's mother, Cordelia represents a difference from the conventional or normal which is both attractive and frightening. Unlike Elaine's mother, however, Cordelia has "power over" (113) Elaine. I suggest that this power lies in the wonderfully imaginative quality of Cordelia's girlhood plots, a quality that helps to shape Elaine's own imagination and contributes to Elaine's decision to pursue a career as an artist rather than a biologist. The unusual complexity of Cordelia's fantasy enters the foreground when she dresses Elaine as Mary Queen of Scots, "headless already" (107), she insists, before her interment. Of course her very name invokes the world of drama, and Elaine clarifies that as a young adult Cordelia "is like someone making herself up as she goes along. She's improvising" (301).

STILL MORE MIRRORS

If this ability to avoid the conventional by reference to what the imagination declares possible is integral to Cordelia's personality, then it is also at the centre of Elaine's, for these two figures undergo mirroring experiences whereby they exchange identities. As usual, Atwood codes the process to mirror imagery. Together Cordelia and Elaine indulge in horror comics as teenagers, their favourite of which describes two sisters, one conventionally beautiful and the other scarred over half of her face. Through a supernatural narcissism, the scarred sister becomes the other as the other gazes into a mirror, and the imposter then wins the handsome suitor. Elaine confides in her autobiography that she fears this will happen to her. "I'm not afraid of seeing Cordelia," she realizes, "I'm afraid of being Cordelia" (227).

On the novel's final pages, Toronto itself becomes linked with Cordelia; it is a place which, Elaine knows, "still has power [to move her]; like a mirror that shows you only the ruined half of your face" (410). That ruined half is perhaps the absent, possibly insane Cordelia, the one person Elaine needs to meet. "I reach out my arms to her" (419), Elaine declares, though she does not in fact see Cordelia again.

One other confrontation in the novel recalls Cordelia, however: Elaine's meeting with a homeless woman to whom she gives money. This woman, who has "green" eyes — "Cordelia's" (153) — shocks Elaine when her response to Elaine's charity is "'I know about you. ... You're Our Lady and you don't love me'"(153). The figure of "Our Lady" is among the most frequently occurring and significant images in this novel, as evidenced by its placement at the moment of Elaine's escape from death by freezing. That figure signals the start of Elaine's escape from Cordelia's power to harm her, too, and yet in the short speech of the street-woman, the Madonna and Cordelia rather than the Madonna and Elaine are combined. Cordelia's formidable powers indeed seem linked to the extraordinary, the supra-rational, and in exchanging identities with her confidante Elaine usurps those powers. She thrives as a painter. She also abandons Cordelia, who disappears into an oblivion like that from which Elaine emerges at age eight when this narrative begins.

Thus Elaine seems a collage of the prominent traits of the shaping women in her life. While she does not make such a revelation explicit in the text, she muses in the end upon what she has just been able to acknowledge as the lack in her life. Having finally brought to consciousness the repressed memories of her childhood traumas, she can again feel the full range of her emotions. On the airplane *en route* to her Vancouver home after the retrospective and her unscheduled visit to the scenes of her greatest childhood traumas, Elaine realizes, looking at the people in the seats next to hers, "[t]his is what I miss,

Cordelia: not something that's gone, but something that will never happen. Two old women giggling over their tea" (421). But Elaine has brought herself to this position; or, as Elaine might put things, "it serves her right." She refused to help Cordelia when Cordelia needed her, acting much as the calculating Mrs. Smeath might have acted. She turned her energies single-mindedly to her work, evading as far as possible the roles of wife and mother, as her own mother would perhaps have done. And she incorporated Cordelia's lively, imaginative mind in her own art.

Elaine's reunion with her past is salutary but without political significance. No political activists appear in *Cat's Eye*. Although the heroine has achieved a stable, fulfilling relationship with a man, neither she nor he is distinctly Canadian in any way. And their indifference to issues of Canadian nationalism — the power of Canada as an economic and political entity — is perhaps a prediction along the same lines as the Canadian federal election of 1988 in which the government was delivered a mandate to pursue economic union with the United States.

WILDERNESS TIPS

The women who appear in Atwood's works of the early 1990s are familiar Atwoodian characterizations, as *Wilderness Tips* reviewer Sherrill Grace points out.[8] While it would be comforting to believe that her 1990s' characters had found their most human and most revolutionary voices, they have not; these women and men inhabit a dark world indeed, as reviewers Aamer Hussein, John Bemrose, and Daniel Jones, for example, agree.[9] In that way they recall the persona of *Interlunar*, noted at the beginning of this chapter, who is "without power" and has "the power of waiting merely."

While the range of occupations and attitudes of the female figures populating the short stories in *Wilderness Tips* could be seen as encouragingly wide, few figures are effectively politicized; some, however, retain hope, the quality Atwood still seems to associate with the possibility of change. The occupations of the central women in the ten stories include lawyer, newspaper columnist, freelance writer, editor of a fashionable Toronto magazine, poet, talk show host, business woman, and money manager. Their affective arrangements show less diversity and are generally dissatisfying to them, just one being shown in a stable relationship. Thus generally they resemble their Atwoodian forebears in achieving worldly success without having changed either the world or the definition of "success" in that world, or without their personal lives having satisfied them. But mirroring experiences persist in these stories, and with them both fruitful inner transformations and the ability to imagine a more compassionate, "Canadian" world.

Kat in "Hairball" can perhaps stand in for other female characters in these pieces with her exaggerated narcissistic experience at the story's end. To arrive at this turning point she has mutated into the opposite of her mother's creation of her: "During her childhood she was a romanticized Katherine, dressed by her misty-eyed, fussy mother in dresses that looked like ruffled pillowcases,"[10] after which she becomes, successively, Kathy, Kath, and now Kat, "the latest thing, hard and shiny, purple-mouthed, crop-headed ... in a little crotch-hugger skirt and skin-tight leggings" (45). She has been dumped and fired by her former lover, who takes her job as editor after having allowed himself to be made over by Kat, for "[h]e likes mirrors" (43). Kat then undergoes a difficult but necessary self-discovery while contemplating her benign ovarian cyst, ensconced on her mantelpiece. Finally, she decides to create yet another new name for herself to signal, perhaps, a journey toward psychic understanding.

The women who play central roles in the last three stories in this collection will define my subject because of their direct connections with other female characters studied here, connections based on their relationships either with another woman or with a sympathetic or unsympathetic man. Atwood's treatment of progressive narcissism as a condition from which positive change might be worked for has all but disappeared, although her commitment to belief in such a condition will be seen to remain.

WEIGHT

The no-name female lawyer turned entrepreneur who narrates this piece has explicitly rejected the feminist agenda planned by her and her law school friend, Molly, an activist eventually bludgeoned to death by her deranged husband. The no-name protagonist and Molly had planned to decode the masculinist language of their profession and so renew it, but the protagonist admits frankly that she has given up. Left to fight for change without the protagonist's help, Molly had, for example, continued to accept as clients women who could not afford to pay her. The protagonist castigates Molly's beliefs, even as she continues to solicit donations for Molly's Place, a home for battered women. Her own ideological and personal state therefore seems as contradictory and unexamined as such earlier Atwoodian females as Rennie Wilford before her mirroring experience late in *Bodily Harm*.

Even the privileged position of "creative non-victim" described in Atwood's early literary criticism[11] here comes under obvious attack. While the newspapers describe Molly as a victim, the speaker declares that she was not: it was precisely her hope, and her faith that her husband's condition would improve, that enabled her to be murdered, the narrator claims. This lack of empathy for her friend's beliefs shows in a similar — and recognizable — lack of emotional commitment in general. Wary of "the risk" (186) of marriage, this middle-aged woman has also recently grown fearful of being alone. Her series of affairs no longer seems enough.

A sombre tale, lacking in mirror imagery, "Weight" ends with the main character planning a kind of eulogy to Molly, a form of testament to female friendship, but here involving only material values. Concerned about middle-aged spread, the protagonist looks forward to a weekend power walk through a local cemetery, when she will pretend that one of the tombstones is Molly's:

> I'll pick out a tombstone where I can do my leg stretches, and I'll pretend it's hers. Molly, I'll say. We don't see eye to eye on some things and you wouldn't approve of my methods, but I do what I

> can. The bottom line is that cash is cash, and it puts food on the table. ... I will bend, I will touch the ground, or as close to it as I can get without rupture. I will lay a wreath of invisible money on her grave. (193)

Immensely concerned about how she looks, for her face and body have won her large donations to the Molly's Place fund, she still wants some intangible, non-material connection with a woman who once meant something to her. That she can only offer money to the friend's memory seems telling.

Thus, hopes for an alternative ethic of community involving mutual emotional and material aid, pertaining to Atwood's women in, for example, *Two-Headed Poems*, are a thing of the past. To attempt to uphold such an ethic in this short story is indeed to open oneself to an early and violent death. Molly's husband Curtis loses control over Molly in his paranoid fantasies and must re-establish his power over her, as previous Atwoodian males have needed to assert control, in this instance by clubbing his wife to death with a claw hammer and distributing her body parts around the city of Toronto.

WILDERNESS TIPS

Mirror imagery reappears here, perhaps signalling the re-emergence of a thematic of hope that will appear in the last story in this volume ("Hack Wednesday," discussed below). Not a hopeful piece, this title story, on the other hand, has as its main characters a wealthy, ruthless businessman, the naturalized Canadian named George, and a rich and unfeeling southern Ontario woman named Prue. An affair between them introduces George to Prue's innocent youngest sister, Portia, whom George marries. A late scene shows Portia finding George making love to Portia's other sister, Pamela.

One of the gentle innocents of Atwood's earlier work, like Aunt Lou in *Lady Oracle*, for example, Portia believes in people, allowing even her own husband to lie constantly about his affairs. She realizes, however, that "[t]here are those who lie by instinct and those who don't, and the ones who don't are at the mercy of the ones who do";

her sister Prue, for instance, "is a blithe liar" (215). Certainly at her husband's and sister's mercy, Portia meets with an attack from her sister Prue when Prue realizes that George has finally gone for the one remaining sister. Prue critizes Portia because she would never "fight back" (220), permitting her mother to marry her off to George.

In a kind of reversal of patterns established by Atwood's earlier women, in which connections with their mothers are repressed (Marian and the narrator of *Surfacing*, for example), Portia seems not to have separated herself from her maternal line. She uses the same expression her mother would have used to attempt to silence Prue — "There's no need to be nasty" (219) — but without success. Her maternal heritage has left her powerless, she realizes: "She wishes she could go back a few decades, grow up again"; "[t]his time she would ... be less obedient; she would not ask for permission. She would not say 'I do' but 'I am'" (219-220). With Prue's assessment of her that she has "always been too good for words" fresh in her mind, Portia then discovers her husband with her eldest sister having sex in the boat-house at their family's lodge, and she wanders off to her old favourite beach to begin her mirroring experience.

In an abbreviated version of a baptism, reminiscent of the one experienced by the narrator in *Surfacing*, Portia strips naked after having slept on the sand and awakened "with pine needles sticking to her cheek" (220-221):

> She wades into the lake, slipping into the water as if between the layers of a mirror: the glass layer, the silver layer. She meets the doubles of her own legs, her own arms, going down. She floats with only her head above water. She is herself at fifteen, herself at twelve, herself at nine, at six. ... It's safe to be this age, to know that the stump is her stump [on shore], the rock is hers, that nothing will ever change. (221)

Knowing that "something bad is about to happen" (221) when she returns to the lodge for dinner and confronts her husband and sisters, she fantasizes herself as someone capable of issuing warnings of impending disaster, a seer. Perhaps with the new knowledge gained from her narcissistic experience in the lake, she can break the pattern of her victimization by husband and family.

HACK WEDNESDAY

Less vulnerable, more powerful, but weary and jaded, the main female figure in the last story in this volume, a columnist for a major Toronto newspaper billed as "a national institution of sorts" (232), Marcia indeed resembles her Atwoodian forebear Rennie Wilford of *Bodily Harm*, though with a pleasing sense of irony. Described by reviewer James Wilcox as "one of Ms. Atwood's most appealing characters,"[12] Marcia is happily married to a left-nationalist Canadian; she persists in writing socially relevant pieces for the newspaper in spite of its new editor, a young man interested in impressing big businessmen in order to show large profits. She feels her days there are numbered owing to the nature of her work:

> she believes, in what she considers to be an old-fashioned, romantic way, that life is something that happens to individuals, despite the current emphasis on statistics and trends. Lately things have taken a grimmer turn in Marcia's column: there's been more about such things as malnutrition in kindergartens, wife-beating, overcrowding in prisons, child abuse. How to behave if you have a friend with AIDS. Homeless people who ask for hand-outs at the entrances to subway stations.
>
> Ian [the new editor] does not like this new slant of Marcia's. (235)

Her political activist husband Eric, an anti-American like his forerunners in Atwood's writing, refuses "to purchase anything from south of the border" since the "Free Trade deal with the States went through" (228); yet she senses that he is wearing out in his angry passions, as she is. "She used to think she had some kind of power" (243), but now, in contrast, "[s]he must watch this tendency to give up, she must get herself under control" (243).

The image that both opens and closes the story is of Marcia's longing, not for more power or drive, but for motherhood, surprising in a collection peopled with childless women. With her two grown children about to visit for Christmas, she dreams in the first paragraph "about babies. She dreams there is a new one, hers. ... She is suffused with love, and with longing for it" (225). To end the story, Marcia will drink spiked eggnog and "she will cry silently to herself, shut into the bathroom and hugging in her festive arms the grumbling cat." She cries over the fact that her children have grown up, that she is no longer a child, that some children have never been children, and that she herself cannot have another child because she is too old. "It's all this talk of babies, at Christmas. It's all this hope. She gets distracted by it, and has trouble paying attention to the real news" (246-247).

Like the luck that seems to sustain Rennie Wilford *en route* to Canada at the end of *Bodily Harm*, this "hope" feeds Marcia at crucial moments. Although she is without power, she has some love — though not the maternal kind of which she dreams — and she is allowed, in what seems a unique moment in Atwood's fiction, to feel "happy" (245). How she and her sister character Elaine Risley from *Cat's Eye*, as well as the healer and saint from her most recent poetry, might feel if power and love were effectively joined, if the accomplishments and successes in their careers and lives seemed less precarious, Atwood seems unwilling or unable, in the early 1990s, to imagine. But by recognizing the continual presence throughout Atwood's work of progressively narcissistic experiences, her readers can perhaps conclude that she has not given up.

TOWARD A PROGRESSIVE NATIONALISM

CANADIANS, including Margaret Atwood, face the economic and other national and international crises that have propelled Canada toward further union with the United States, and Atwood, like her own protagonists, as well as many of her intellectual colleagues in Canada, wonders if such union can be avoided. While she seems to believe it can, Canadian writer Rick Salutin comments forebodingly on "the illogical, unlikely project of existing on this continent in the face of and separate from the United States":

> A non-imperialistic, non-mighty, non-ideological nation. As a country we were always improbable: why didn't the Americans just take us over? Now that they might ... the fact that they were prevented before now starts to loom as a considerable feat. Once Canada is gone, won't we look back and feel, *It's rather impressive that they kept it from happening for as long as they did.*[1]

But the very improbability, the imaginative and philosophical leaps Canadians have had to make for Canada to have persevered as long as it has still encourage Atwood, as the conclusion to her detailed and thoughtful contribution to *If You Love This Country* witnesses: "Our national animal is the beaver, noted for its industry and its co-operative spirit. In medieval bestiaries it is also noted for its habit, when frightened, of biting off its own testicles and offering them to its pursuer. I hope we are not succumbing to some form of that impulse."[2]

Atwood's persistent hopefulness perhaps serves to underscore the idea that regressive narcissism — loss of a sense of history and of compassion for others — is a condition affecting males most deeply, and that males might be freed from the pathology by a kind of woman whose psychic journey has issued in a progressive definition of human power. Supporting the psychoanalytic frame through which I study Atwood's women and men, Canadians and Americans, in terms of their concept of self, is the underlying fact of international history and politics. A character's conception of nationality is determined in much the same way as the character's conception of positioning within a family: Atwood seems to ask, as she limns her personae, what kind of subjects Canada has produced as a colonized country whose identity has, until the past quarter-century, been allied more with the position of the child than the parent. Having avoided "adulthood," she responds, Canada has also avoided a pathological narcissism resulting from fear of declining patriarchal authority. Canada also, however, seems near a failure to displace narcissistic subjects with those who use power in more humanitarian ways, thereby redefining and redistributing it. Hence, the cultural mirror of her writing has shown individual women achieving psychological integrity and power through reclaiming their maternal histories, while her writing has failed to show any kind of similar communal reclamation.

But as Canada has come of age, so has North American feminism, and it might now be possible to see for Canada a future in which its "adult" state is no longer male in any conventional sense, nor conventionally female as Atwood has defined traditional Canadian femaleness — admirably modest and vulnerable but also ineffective on its own. The mature Canadian state might in fact produce subjects who avoid many of the limitations of North American identity as it has been conventionally defined: a continent seen as male and capitalist-imperialist because of the dominance of the United States might instead be seen as female and socialist-nationalist when viewed from a Canadian perspective.

Canada is facing critical decisions as its independence from the

United States seems imperilled. In keeping with this fact, Atwood's future writing may show male and female characters who, unlike the Canadian diplomat or Rennie herself in *Bodily Harm*, can go beyond mainstream thinking to forge a language in which a feminist-socialist Canadian perspective can be maintained and its distinctive influence felt. Atwood's new work may continue, that is, to encode her idea of Canadianness and to promote a future not only for "Canadian" writing but also for the wider culture such writing mirrors and helps to create.

To retrace the progress of Atwood's fictional women, with a view to the future: the mirror stage of the 1970s resulted in female characters who seemed to have discovered a community of love and work after having turned temporarily away from dominant men in their lives, toward other women, especially mothers, sisters, and aunts. Their transformation showed itself in a richer inner life, one that reconnected them with their own histories of vulnerability. That history was figured as both Canadian and feminist, and so when the central female speakers emerged from the mirror stage they spoke in a newly acquired voice, a voice giving preference to acceptance of change and to understanding of human limitations and the consequent need for interdependence. These female figures thus came to embody precisely the balance between relationship and separation that Carol Gilligan describes in *In a Different Voice*.

The fact that the female protagonists who follow Joan Foster of *Lady Oracle* and the speaker in *Two-Headed Poems* in Atwood's work of the 1980s and 1990s experience their transformations in isolation, failing to find in their milieux other women and men who speak the same language of compassion and hope for the marginal, strikes a sobering note in Atwood's later work. But Canadian feminism, and relatedly the chance for a renewed nationalism, survive in shadowy form in her fiction, although her protagonists have troubled relationships with the feminist movement. Consider the remarks of Elaine Risley of *Cat's Eye*, for example, when assessing her feelings toward the women — feminists — who have organized her retrospective and who manage the art gallery where it is held: "I should be grateful, these women are on my side. ... But I still feel outnumbered, as if they are a species of which I am not a member."[3] Consider, too, the ambivalence of the unnamed narrator of "Weight" in *Wilderness Tips* to the leftist-feminist ideology of her murdered law school classmate, Molly:

> Molly, I let you down. I burned out early. I couldn't take the pressure. I wanted security. Maybe I decided that the fastest way to improve the lot of women was to improve my own.
>
> Molly kept on ... She began to lecture me about my lack of seriousness, and also about my wardrobe, for which I overspent in her opinion. She began to use words like *patriarchy*. I began to find her strident.
>
> "Molly," I said. "Why don't you give it up? You're slamming your head against a big brick wall." ... Molly was knocking herself out, and for peanuts. The kind of women she represented never had any money.
>
> "We're making progress," she'd say. ... "We're accomplishing something."
>
> "Who is this *we?*" I'd say. "I don't see a lot of people helping you out."
>
> "Oh, they do," she said vaguely.[4]

But those feminist communities exist, if only on the margins of Atwood's fictional world, and in those communities persists the kind of personality Marilyn French calls for in *Beyond Power*, one that has been so influenced by feminism that it values "love and compassion and sharing and nutritiveness equally with control and structure, possession and status."[5] To order one's life with such ideals in mind is to learn a subversive, poetic language, to refer to Kristevan vocabulary, a language made obvious in speech that, through its unconventionality, upsets the existing paternal, Symbolic order by recalling an Imaginary, maternal phase prior to language and its hierarchies. Such fruitful journeys back, forming an obsessive pattern in Atwood's work, seem to point to the possibility of feminist efficacy in a world that needs the visions of innovative emerging political thinkers.

The Canadian state, along with others worldwide, has undergone and will inevitably undergo revision and realignment. Who will direct that revision seems less clear. Atwood's writing has more or less explicitly shown that Canadian women, especially those who value a socialist ethic, might be admirably suited for such a task, and in so arguing, Atwood steps outside of mainstream Canadian political thinking. But for her most radical voice to be recognized and heeded, and for her work to continue to mirror a hope for progressive change, she — like her protagonists and readers — may need to witness the formation of alliances that similarly speak from the margins. And, as Offred of *The Handmaid's Tale* assures, "there will always be alliances."[6]

Atwood's Canadian women have not yet found an adequate language to propagate their left-nationalism, but they may still do so. Julia Kristeva's analysis of shifting national and ideological boundaries in the late twentieth century, in her *Nations Without Nationalism*, claims that women, who "have the luck and the responsibility of being boundary-subjects," must play a crucial role in promoting the heterogeneity that will characterize newly ordered nations:

> The maturity of the second sex will be judged in coming years according to its ability to modify the nation in the face of foreigners, to orient foreigners confronting the nation toward a still unforeseeable conception of a polyvalent community.[7]

Grounded particularly in knowledge of French history, Kristeva's view of a progressive nationalism demands tolerance of difference, from both old-stock citizens and more recent arrivals alike. Such an attitude seems particularly suited to a *fin de siècle* Canadian nationalism also, one that must acknowledge not only Americanization but also increasing economic globalization.

Atwood's untiring defence of a Canadian way that is feminist, egalitarian, and humane may indeed find a powerful and authentic voice in her work to come. The voice may differ somewhat from her earlier nationalistic personae, given the world alterations the speaker has witnessed and been changed by, but what may remain constant is that the work in which s/he appears will be studied. For Atwood's many readers may well include those who have inherited, or are about to inherit, the power to form this newly emerging world.

❖

NOTES

INTRODUCTION

1. Margaret Atwood, "Notes on Power Politics," *Acta Victoriana*, 97, 2 (1973), 16.

2. Beryl Donaldson Langer, "Class and Gender in Margaret Atwood's Fiction," *Australian-Canadian Studies*, 6, 1 (1988), 98, 74.

3. Donna Haraway, *Primate Vision: Gender, Race, and Nature in the World of Modern Science* (New York: Routledge, 1989), 292.

4. References to Canada are to English Canada except when French Canada is specified.

5. Bob White, *If You Love This Country: Facts and Feelings on Free Trade*, ed. Laurier LaPierre (Report 1988; Toronto: McClelland and Stewart, 1987), 69. White's essay, like the others in this volume, is untitled. Atwood's is the lead piece, and all are "essential reading for anyone concerned about the future of Canada," to quote from the back cover. One of the most interesting characteristics of this collection is the repetition of terms such as "dream," "aspiration," "hope," and "faith" to modify the writers' views of the Canadian difference, terms which recur in Atwood's vision of Canada.

6. David Crane, *If You Love This Country*, 102.

7. Pierre Berton, *If You Love This Country*, 26.

8. Donaldson Langer is an exception (see note 2 above) among Atwood's critics for her neutral assessment of Atwood's treatment of class. Historical materialist critic James Steele, for example, criticizes Atwood's thematic guide to Canadian literature, *Survival*, because it "manages to modify only slightly [Northrop] Frye's idealist liberal and cosmopolitan understanding of the social genesis of literature," "The Literary Criticism of Margaret Atwood," in *In Our*

Own House, ed. Paul Cappon (Toronto: McClelland and Stewart, 1978), 78. Larry MacDonald asserts that "nowhere, in any of the novels by these writers [Atwood, Hugh MacLennan, and Robertson Davies], does left-nationalism appear as anything but the babblings of psychological misfits," "Psychologism and the Philosophy of Progress," *Studies in Canadian Literature* 9,2 (1984), 133. Kenneth Hoeppner, however, argues that Frye's mythopoeic structuralism is not apolitical and indeed provides the most appropriate methodology for analysing Atwood's novel *Surfacing*, "The Political Implications of Literature," diss., University of Calgary, 1984. (When working toward her honours B.A. at University of Toronto's Victoria College Atwood of course studied with Frye.) Rick Salutin, on the other hand, interprets Atwood's *Survival* as compatible with historical materialist criticism, concluding that "the analysis of literature in *Survival* leads to the necessity of political action in society," "A Note on the Marxism of Atwood's *Survival*," *The Malahat Review*, 41 (1977), 60. None of these critics links her successful or failed Marxism with her feminism.

9. Beryl Donaldson Langer, "Interview with Margaret Atwood," *Australian-Canadian Studies*, 6, 1 (1988), 130. For treatment of Canada's three main political parties, see Bell and Tepperman, Brown, Christian, Newman, Penner, and Thorburn in the Canadian History section of my Works Consulted.

10. Rachel Blau DuPlessis has written that Atwood herself, as a Canadian and a woman, is twice removed from the dominant North American order, creating the conditions for Atwood's "double marginalization." In Atwood and the other writers in similar conditions whom DuPlessis treats, their double marginalization "[e]ither ... compels the person to negate any possibility for a critical stance ... or it enlivens the potential for critique by the production of an (ambiguously) nonhegemonic person, one in marginalized dialogue with the orders she may also affirm," in her *Writing Beyond the Ending* (Bloomington, IN: Indiana University Press, 1985), 33.

11. Robert Kroetsch, "Unhiding the Hidden," *Journal of Canadian Fiction*, 3, 3 (1974), 44, an essay reprinted in *Open Letter*. Fifth series, 4 (Spring 1983), 17-21, an issue entitled "Robert Kroetsch: Essays" and edited by Frank Davey and bp Nichol.

12. Margaret Homans, "'Her Very Own Howl,'" *Signs*, 9, 2 (1983), 196.

13. Coral Ann Howells writes that a distinctively Canadian treatment of the convergence of feminism and nationalism occurs in the eleven writers she discusses in her *Private and Fictional Words* (London, UK: Methuen, 1987), although

she does not define "nationalism" or "feminism" closely in Atwood's terms in the chapter devoted to Atwood's *Bodily Harm* and *The Handmaid's Tale*. In that section Howells does, however, like me, situate Atwood as a theorist of power.

14. Margaret Atwood, "Notes on Power Politics," *Acta Victoriana*, 97, 2 (1973), 16.

15. For a text that should be read in conjunction with the other Canadian histories quoted here, see Alison Prentice, et al., *Canadian Women: A History* (Toronto: Harcourt, Brace, Jovanovich, 1988).

CHAPTER ONE

1. Atwood's concern with ideas of power is witnessed first in the subject of her unfinished Harvard Ph.D. thesis, "Nature and Power in the English Metaphysical Romance of the Nineteenth and Twentieth Centuries." Its two major subdivisions are "The Power of Nature" and "The Nature of Power." This manuscript is housed with her other papers at the Thomas Fisher Rare Book Library, University of Toronto. Atwood continues to attend to power in a volume devoted to it, *Power Politics* (Toronto: Anansi, 1971), and less explicitly throughout her work.

2. See Alicia Suskin Ostriker, *Stealing the Language* (Boston: Beacon, 1986) in which she argues that the voice of woman has in the past been "trapped by her own gentleness, by her own avoidance of power" (138). See Carol P. Christ, *Diving Deep and Surfacing* (Boston: Beacon, 1980) where she states that "[m]any women seek new visions of power and personhood and do not wish simply to become like men in their struggle for equality and justice" (11). See Claire Keyes, *The Aesthetics of Power: The Poetry of Adrienne Rich* (Athens, GA: University of Georgia, 1986) in which references to Rich's understanding of feminist as opposed to patriarchal power appear in each of the book's ten chapters.

3. Mirrors and narcissism have received considerable treatment by Atwood's critics, although few link the two and none further ties them to Canadian nationalism. I give a name to Atwood's sense of a new narcissism, contextualize it, and trace its relationship to mirror imagery in her work. My study thus builds upon and is indebted to all of the existing criticism treating mirrors and narcissism in Atwood's texts. For studies that combine attention to narcissism and the figure of the mirror see: Frank Davey, *Margaret Atwood* (Vancouver:

Talonbooks, 1984), 97; Lorna Irvine, "The Red and Silver Heroes Have Collapsed," *Concerning Poetry*, 12 (Fall 1979), 65; Gloria Onley, "Power Politics in Bluebeard's Castle," *Canadian Literature*, 60 (Spring 1974), 25-26, 29; Jerome Rosenberg, *Margaret Atwood* (Boston: Twayne, 1984), 24, 27; Barbara Blakely, "The Pronunciation of Flesh: A Feminist Reading of Margaret Atwood's Poetry," in *Margaret Atwood*, ed. Sherrill E. Grace and Lorraine Weir (Vancouver: University of British Columbia, 1983), 35. Francis Mansbridge studies mirrors and narcissism without linking them in his "Search for Self in the Novels of Margaret Atwood," *Journal of Canadian Fiction*, 22 (1978), 109.

For studies of narcissism in Atwood's writing, see: Catherine Rainwater, "The Sense of the Flesh in Four Novels by Margaret Atwood," in *Margaret Atwood*, ed. Beatrice Mendez-Egle (Edinburg, TX: Pan American University Press, 1987), 17; Rosemary Sullivan, "Breaking the Circle," *The Malahat Review*, 41 (January 1977), 32; Sharon R. Wilson, "The Fragmented Self in *Lady Oracle*," *Commonwealth Novel in English*, 1 (January 1982), 72; John Lauber, "Alice in Consumer-Land," in *The Canadian Novel*, ed. John Moss (Toronto: New Canada Press, 1978), 24; Francis Mansbridge, who reads recent Canadian fiction in general with reference to narcissism in his "Narcissism in the Modern Canadian Novel," *Studies in Canadian Literature*, 6, 1 (1981), 232.

For studies of mirror imagery and mirroring in Atwood's writing, see: Russell M. Brown, "Atwood's Sacred Wells," *Essays on Canadian Writing*, 17 (Spring 1980), 33; Nora Foster Stovel, "Reflections on Mirror Images," *Essays on Canadian Writing*, 33 (Fall 1986), 50; Kathryn VanSpanckeren, "Magic in the Novels of Margaret Atwood," in *Margaret Atwood*, ed. Beatrice Mendez-Egle, 9; Catherine Sheldrick Ross, "'Banished To This Other Place,'" *English Studies in Canada*, 6 (Winter 1980), 467; the following three — Sherrill E. Grace, "Articulating the 'Space Between'" (11), Philip Stratford, "The Uses of Ambiguity" (113), and Lorraine Weir, "Atwood in a Landscape" (142), in *Margaret Atwood*, ed. Sherrill E. Grace and Lorraine Weir; Maureen Dilliott, "Emerging from the Cold," *Modern Poetry Studies*, 8 (Spring 1977), 79; John Wilson Foster, "The Poetry of Margaret Atwood," *Canadian Literature*, 74 (Autumn 1977), 13; the following five — Judith McCombs, "Atwood's Haunted Sequences" (47, 52), Sherrill E. Grace, "Margaret Atwood and the Poetics of Duplicity" (56), Lorraine Weir, "Meridians of Perception" (69), Linda W. Wagner, "The Making of Selected Poems" (86), Robert Lecker, "Janus through the Looking Glass" (178), in *The Art of Margaret Atwood*, ed. Arnold E. Davidson and Cathy N. Davidson (Toronto: Anansi, 1981); Barbara Godard, "My (m)Other, My Self," *Essays on Canadian Writing*, 26 (Summer 1983), 17, 20, 24; Linda Sandler, "Preface," "Margaret Atwood: A

Symposium," ed. Linda Sandler, *The Malahat Review*, 41 (January 1977), 5; Barbara C. Ewell, "The Language of Alienation in Margaret Atwood's *Surfacing*," *The Centennial Review*, 25 (Spring 1981), 199; Susan Maclean, "*Lady Oracle*," *Journal of Canadian Fiction*, 28/29 (1980), 185; Lucy M. Freibert, "The Artist as Picaro," *Canadian Literature*, 92 (Spring 1982), 31-32; Barbara Hill Rigney devotes the final two chapters of her *Madness and Sexual Politics in the Feminist Novel* (Madison, WI: University of Wisconsin Press, 1978) to strategies of mirroring and doubling in Atwood's work; Jessie Givner, "Mirror Images in Margaret Atwood's *Lady Oracle*," *Studies in Canadian Literature*, 41, 1 (1989), 141.

4. Coral Ann Howells argues that a distinctively Canadian treatment of the convergence of feminism and nationalism occurs in the eleven writers she discusses in her *Private and Fictional Words* (London, UK: Methuen, 1987). The third chapter treating Atwood's *Bodily Harm* and *The Handmaid's Tale* supports my reading of Atwood as a theorist of power.

5. My definition of "narcissism" is psychoanalytic, not the popular cultural meaning of "narcissism" as "vanity." For a distinction between the two and a defence of vanity as a revolutionary force in the underclasses, see Stanley Aronowitz, "On Narcissism," *Telos*, 44 (Summer 1980), 65-74. His essay appears in the section "Special Symposium on Narcissism" where Kovel's essay noted below also appears. The section contains papers from the Cortland Conference on Narcissism, State University of New York-Cortland 3-5 April 1980.

6. Joel Kovel, "Narcissism and the Family," *Telos*, 44 (Summer 1980), 91.

7. For a provocative Lacanian reading of Canadian sociopolitical history see Tony Wilden, *The Imaginary Canadian* (Vancouver: Pulp Press, 1980), in which Wilden argues that Canadians, like children, have accepted an identity and sense of power given them by the "adult," parent countries Britain, France, and the US. To determine what is indigenously Canadian, we must reinterpret our own history and culture from our perspective, allowing us finally "to take whatever we need from wherever we find it from whatever tradition" (118). Wilden has translated and written notes and commentary to Lacan's *Speech and Language in Psychoanalysis* (Baltimore, MD: Johns Hopkins University Press, 1968).

8. Deborah Silverton Rosenfelt, "Feminism, 'Postfeminism,' and Contemporary Women's Fiction," in *Tradition and the Talents of Women*, ed. Florence Howe (Urbana, IL: University of Illinois Press, 1991), 268-291. References to Atwood's *The Handmaid's Tale* as a postfeminist text appear on pp. 282-283.

9. Sneja Gunew, "Framing Marginality," *Southern Review* [Adelaide], 18 (1985), 145, 155, 151. See also Sneja Gunew, ed., *A Reader in Feminist Knowledge* (London, UK: Routledge, 1991).

10. *Nationalisms and Sexualities*, ed. Andrew Parker et al. (New York: Routledge, 1992), 3.

11. Elizabeth Janeway, *Powers of the Weak* (Knopf, 1980; New York: Morrow Quill Paperbacks, 1981), 157.

12. Jacques Lacan, "The mirror stage," in his *Ecrits: A Selection*, trans. Alan-Sheridan (New York: W.W. Norton, 1977), 1-7.

13. Joseph H. Smith, *Arguing with Lacan* (New Haven, CT: Yale University Press, 1991), 62-63.

14. Linda Sandler, "Interview with Margaret Atwood," *The Malahat Review*, 41 (January 1977), 24. Elsewhere Atwood adds that "the literary culture, as a whole, often acts like a mirror of the society," Karla Hammond, "An Interview with Margaret Atwood," *The American Poetry Review*, 8, 5 (1979), 27. Of current Afro-American women writers in the US, writers among the burgeoning of their culture as are current Canadian writers, Atwood states: they "think it's important that a people be able to see its own reflection in the mirror of art, and they see art very much as a mirror," in her *Second Words* (Boston: Beacon, 1984), 360. Quite early in her public career Atwood wrote: "Poetry isn't a sermon or a solution or even an analysis. But sometimes it's a reflection. We use the reflections of ourselves in mirrors so we can see what we look like. If the sight is too horrible we sometimes make efforts to change it. But with no recognition there can be no change," in "Notes on Power Politics," *Acta Victoriana*, 97 (April 1973), 7.

15. Christopher Lasch, *The Culture of Narcissism* (New York: W.W. Norton, 1978), 10. For worthwhile commentary on Lasch's work, see "A Symposium: Christopher Lasch and the Culture of Narcissism," *Salmagundi*, 46 (Fall 1979), 166-202; Lasch's own "What's Wrong with the Right," *Tikkun*, 1, 1 (1986), 23-29; and another symposium, "Christopher Lasch and Critics on The Family," *Tikkun*, 1, 2 (1986), 85-97.

   In a telephone conversation 11 August 1986, Atwood remarked to me that she is well aware of Lasch's work, although she has not read it systematically. Lasch, however, has read Atwood's work, as his mention of her *Survival* in a footnote to his *The Minimal Self* indicates (271).

16. Otto F. Kernberg, "Narcissism," in *Introducing Psychoanalytic Theory*, ed. Sander L. Gilman (New York: Brunner/Mazel, 1982), 128. In this essay

Kernberg distinguishes between his work and that of the other major American writer on narcissism, Heinz Kohut. He states, "[i]n contrast to Kohut," whose emphasis is more intrapsychic, "I consider object relations integral to development" (132). Kernberg is thus more nearly allied with object relations psychology and Kohut with self psychology. Kernberg's primary text on narcissism is *Borderline Conditions and Pathological Narcissism* (New York: Jason Aronson, 1975). Kohut's basic text is *The Analysis of the Self* (New York: International Universities Press, 1971). Kernberg clarifies concerning his and Kohut's work that "[b]oth views originally developed from Freud's thinking" (130). The significant Freudian text is "On Narcissism," in *The Standard Edition of the Complete Psychological Works*, ed. James Strachey, vol. XIV, 67-102. See also *Freud's "On Narcissism: An Introduction,"* ed. Joseph Sandler et al. (New Haven, CT: Yale University Press, 1991).

17. Kathleen Woodward, "The Look and the Gaze," Working Paper No. 7 (Milwaukee: University of Wisconsin/Center for Twentieth Century Studies, 1986), 2. She continues, "I refer in particular to Kohut because in the United States his work on narcissism is widely acknowledged to have shifted the emphasis from the theorization of narcissism in negative terms to positive terms" (2). Woodward herself in this paper poses a theory of "benevolent narcissism" as basis for "benevolent relations with others" (12).

18. Christopher Lasch, *The Minimal Self* (New York: W.W.Norton, 1984), 33. Other references to this work will be cited in the text.

19. Jessica Benjamin, "The Oedipal Riddle," in *The Problem of Authority in America*, ed. John P. Diggins and Mark Kann (Philadelphia, PA: Temple University Press, 1981), 198, 209, 219, 209, 207. A more recent essay, building upon these ideas, is Benjamin's "A Desire of One's Own" in *Feminist Studies/Critical Studies*, ed. Teresa de Lauretis (Bloomington, IN: Indiana University Press, 1986), 78-101, in which she proposes an object-relations model of "intersubjectivity" for human development.

20. Hilary M. Lips, *Women, Men, and Power* (Mountain View, CA: Mayfield Publishing, 1991), 10.

21. Marilyn French, *Beyond Power* (New York: Summit, 1985), 76, 334, 387, 443, 454.

22. George Steiner, "The Retreat from the Word," in *George Steiner* (Harmondsworth, UK: Penguin, 1984), 297. His statement squares with a basic belief of Kristevan semiotics, although Steiner does not acknowledge a connection with feminist theory. And Kristeva of course does not share Steiner's Anglo-American intellectual tradition.

23. Carol Gilligan, *In a Different Voice: Psychological Theory and Women's Development* (Cambridge, MA: Harvard University Press, 1982), 173, 63.

24. Carol Gilligan, "On In a Different Voice; An Interdisciplinary Forum," *Signs*, 11, 2 (1986), 331, 333.

25. This is classical Freudian theory as proposed, for example, in "Femininity," in *The Standard Edition of the Complete Psychological Works*, ed. James Strachey, vol. XXII, 112-135.

26. Julia Kristeva, *Desire in Language*, ed. Leon S. Roudiez, trans. Thomas Gora et al. (New York: Columbia University Press, 1980), 31, 65, 70. "Instinctual drives" in the passage quoted at length represent an impulse opposite to the "rationalization" referred to in Benjamin's "The Oedipal Riddle," 216. Development of Kristeva's theories of the feminine and the maternal appear in, for example, her "Stabat Mater," in *The Female Body in Western Culture*, ed. Susan Rubin Suleiman (Cambridge, MA: Harvard University Press, 1986), 99-118; "Women's Time," *Signs*, 7,1 (1981), 13-35 (see also Alice Jardine, "Introduction to Julia Kristeva's 'Women's Time,'" in the same issue of *Signs*, 5-12); "The Maternal Body," *m/f*, 5/6 (1981), 158-163 (see also Claire Pajaczkowska, "Introduction to Kristeva," 149-157 and "Interview-1974: Julia Kristeva and Psychanalyse et Politique," 164-167 in the same issue of *m/f*.) For commentary on Kristeva's work in its French contexts see Elaine Marks, "Women and Literature in France," and Carolyn Greenstein Burke, "Report from Paris," *Signs*, 3,3 (1978), 832-855; "Part II: Contemporary Feminist Thought in France: Translating Difference," in *The Future of Difference*, ed. Hester Eisenstein and Alice Jardine (Boston: G. K. Hall, 1980), 71-121; Toril Moi, "Marginality and Subversion: Julia Kristeva," in her *Sexual/Textual Politics* (London, UK: Methuen, 1985), 150-173; John Lechte, *Julia Kristeva* (London, UK: Routledge, 1990).

27. Atwood, *Second Words* (Boston: Beacon, 1984), 332.

28. Kaja Silverman, *The Acoustic Mirror* (Bloomington, IN: Indiana University Press, 1988), 113, 125.

29. Marianne Hirsch, *The Mother/Daughter Plot* (Bloomington, IN: Indiana University Press, 1989), 145.

30. Kristeva, *Black Sun*, trans. Leon S. Roudiez (Paris, 1987; New York: Columbia University Press, 1989), 14, 43. Kristeva's other works of relevance to my study of language are: *Tales of Love*, trans. Leon S. Roudiez (Paris 1983; New York: Columbia University Press, 1987); *Language the Unknown: An Initiation into Linguistics*, trans. Anne M. Menke (Paris, 1981; New York,

Columbia University Press, 1989); *Strangers to Ourselves*, trans. Leon S. Roudiez (New York: Columbia University Press, 1991).

31. Luce Irigaray, "Women's Exile," trans. Couze Venn, *Ideology and Consciousness*, 1 (1977), 68.

32. "Women's Exile," 75.

33. Irigaray, *Speculum of the Other Woman*, trans. Gillian C. Gill (Ithaca, NY: Cornell University Press, 1985), 205.

34. *Speculum*, 11-129. This quotation forms part of the title of the book's opening section.

35. *Speculum*, 239.

36. Kernberg, "Narcissism," 130.

37. Robert Bothwell et al., *Canada since 1945* (Toronto: University of Toronto Press, 1981). For a spare and lucid discussion of the 1960s and 1970s in North America, see Part Five and Part Six, 267-460. References to this work will be cited in the text by page number.

38. John F. Burns, "A Leftist Leader Surging in Canada," *The New York Times*, 8 November 1987, 1, 8. Burns writes that a "poll published last week by *The Globe and Mail*, a Toronto newspaper, showed Mr. [Ed] Broadbent's [New Democratic] party with 38 percent support nationwide, compared with 35 percent for the Liberals and 24 percent for the governing Conservatives" (1). Broadbent, former leader of the NDP, is quoted as defining the New Democrats as "a 'social democratic party,' not socialist" (8). History of Canada's three major political parties appears in Bothwell et al. Provinces such as Canada's largest anglophone province, Ontario, have elected NDP governments in recent years for the first time.

The following are histories of the social democrats exclusively: David Bell and Lorne Tepperman, *The Roots of Disunity: A Look at Canadian Political Culture* (Toronto: McClelland and Stewart, 1979), especially the first three chapters; William Christian, "Ideology and Politics in Canada," in *Approaches to Canadian Politics*, 2nd ed., ed. John H. Redekop (Scarborough, ON: Prentice-Hall Canada, 1983); Norman Penner, "The Development of Social Democracy in Canada," in *Political Thought in Canada: Contemporary Perspectives*, ed. Stephen Brooks (Toronto: Irwin, 1984); "Section Four: Third Parties," in *Party Politics in Canada*, 5th ed., ed. Hugh G. Thorburn (Scarborough, ON: Prentice-Hall Canada, 1985). But the most significant essay from the field of political science, linking in Atwoodian fashion the efforts of Canadian feminism and social democracy, is Rosemary Brown's "A New Kind of Power," in *Women in the Canadian Mosaic,* ed. Gwen Matheson (Toronto: Peter Martin Associates, 1976), 289-298.

39. Bothwell et al., *Canada since 1945,* 377.

40. Bothwell et al., 392.

41. Mark Nichols, "Canadians Speak Out on Issues and Hopes," *Maclean's,* 4 January 1988, 34.

42. Peter C. Newman, "Bold and Cautious," p. 25 in "Special Report: Portrait of Two Nations," *Maclean's,* 3 July 1989, 23-84.

43. Lawrence Martin, *Pledge of Allegiance* (Toronto: McClelland and Stewart, 1993), 194, 189, 195-6, 246.

44. Margaret Atwood, "Free Traders Don't Eat Quiche," *The Globe and Mail,*17 November 1988, A7.

CHAPTER TWO

1. For general commentary on Atwood's Canada vs. her US, see S. J. Colman, "Margaret Atwood, Lucien Goldmann's Pascal, and the Meaning of 'Canada,'" *University of Toronto Quarterly,* 48, 3 (Spring 1979), 245-262, and Valerie Broege, "Margaret Atwood's Americans and Canadians," *Essays on Canadian Writing,* 22 (Summer 1981), 111-135. See also Atwood, "Canadian-American Relations," in her *Second Words* (Boston: Beacon, 1984).

    Two recent studies of the issue are: Judith McCombs, "Politics, Structure, and Poetic Developement in Atwood's Canadian-American Sequences," 142-162, and June Schlueter, "Canlit/Victimlit: Survival and Second Words," 1-11, both in *Margaret Atwood: Vision and Forms,* ed. Kathryn VanSpanckeren and Jan Garden Castro (Carbondale, IL: Southern Illinois University Press, 1988).

2. Jim Davidson, "Margaret Atwood [interview]," *Meanjin,* 37, 2 (1978), 193-194.

3. "Margaret Atwood," in *Eleven Canadian Novelists Interviewed by Graeme Gibson* (Toronto: Anansi, 1973), 27, 22, 24. Her understanding of Canadian writers' representations of victimization and colonization is thoroughly articulated in her *Survival* (Toronto: Anansi, 1972).

4. Davidson, 196.

5. Julia Kristeva, *Strangers to Ourselves*, trans. Leon S. Roudiez (New York: Columbia University Press, 1991), 2.

6. Atwood uses the term "narcissism" to signify "vanity" as is clear in her essay "Canadian-American Relations" (see note 1 above) when she calls 1970s' Toronto "the Paris of the Northeast ... clean, safe, glitzy, filled with restaurants of high guality, and up to its eyeballs in narcissism" (381).

7. The Canadian/American opposition in *The Edible Woman* is discussed in only one work, Walter Wayne Fraser, "The Dominion of Women," diss., University of Manitoba, 1985. Deconstructive and other philosophical approaches to the first novel include T. D. MacLulich, "Atwood's Adult Fairy Tale," *Essays on Canadian Writing*, 11 (Summer 1978), 124; Lorraine McMullen, "The Divided Self," *Atlantis*, 5, 2 (Spring 1980), 62; Cheryl Stokes Rackowski, "Women by Women," diss., University of Connecticut, 1978, 39; Gloria Onley, "Power Politics in Bluebeard's Castle," *Canadian Literature*, 60 (Spring 1974), 25; Francis Mansbridge, "Search for Self in the Novels of Margaret Atwood," *Journal of Canadian Fiction*, 22 (1978), 109-110; Nora Foster Stovel, "Reflections on Mirror Images," *Essays on Canadian Writing*, 33 (Fall 1986), 53; Esther Robertson argues for a failure of deconstructive logic, "The Politics of Relationships," M.A. Thesis, University of British Columbia, 1974, 16.

8. The literary approaches treating style include Margaret Griffith, "Verbal Terrain in the Novels of Margaret Atwood," *Critique*, 21, 3 (1980), 87; Catherine Rainwater, "The Sense of the Flesh in Four Novels by Margaret Atwood," in *Margaret Atwood*, ed. Beatrice Mendez-Egle (Edinburg, TX: Pan American University Press, 1987), 20. For critics who attend to form and genre see Jayne Patterson, "The Taming of Externals," *Studies in Canadian Literature*, 7, 2 (1982), 156; Sherrill E. Grace, *Violent Duality* (Montreal: Véhicule, 1980), 94; Jerome H. Rosenberg, *Margaret Atwood* (Boston: Twayne, 1984), 102-103; Linda Rogers, "Margaret the Magician," *Canadian Literature*, 60 (Spring 1974), 84; Kathryn VanSpanckeren, "Magic in the Novels of Margaret Atwood," in *Margaret Atwood*, ed. Beatrice Mendez-Egle, 3; Catherine McLay, "The Dark Voyage," in *The Art of Margaret Atwood*, ed. Arnold E. Davidson and Cathy N. Davidson (Toronto: Anansi, 1981), 125; Glenys Stow, "Nonsense as Social Commentary in *The Edible Woman*," *Journal of Canadian Studies*, 23, 3 (1988), 90. Critics evaluating Atwood's writing as art include Frank Davey, "Atwood Walking Backwards," *Open Letter*. 2nd Series, 5 (Summer 1973), 76, and his *Margaret Atwood* (Vancouver: Talonbooks, 1984), 63; Linda Hutcheon, "From Poetic to

Narrative Structures," in *Margaret Atwood*, ed. Sherrill E. Grace and Lorraine-Weir (Vancouver; University of British Columbia Press, 1983), 20.

9. See Elizabeth Brady, "Towards a happier history," in *Domination*, ed.Alkis Kontos (Toronto: University of Toronto Press, 1975), 30; and especially Gayle Greene, "Margaret Atwood's *The Edible Woman*," in *Margaret Atwood*, ed. Beatrice Mendez-Egle, 99, 105.

10. Christopher Lasch, *The Culture of Narcissism* (New York : W.W. Norton, 1978), 10.

11. Otto F. Kernberg, "Narcissism," in *Introducing Psychoanalytic Theory* (New York: Brunner/Mazel, 1982), 135.

12. Atwood, *The Edible Woman* (Toronto: McClelland and Stewart, 1969), 174. Other references to this work will be cited in the text by page number.

13. See Elizabeth Meese, *Crossing the Double Cross* (Chapel Hill, NC: University of North Carolina Press, 1986), 124; Robert Kroetsch, "Unhiding the Hidden," *Journal of Canadian Fiction*, 3, 3 (1974), 43; Barbara Hill Rigney, *Madness and Sexual Politics in the Feminist Novel* (Madison, WI: University of Wisconsin Press, 1978), 111; Robert Lecker, "Janus through the Looking Glass," in *The Art of Margaret Atwood*, ed. Arnold E. Davidson and Cathy N. Davidson (Toronto: Anansi, 1981), 188; Sherrill E. Grace, "Articulating the 'Space Between'" in *Margaret Atwood*, ed. Sherrill E. Grace and Lorraine Weir (Vancouver: University of British Columbia Press, 1983), 5; Susan Beckman, "Language as Cultural Identity in Achebe, Ihimaera, Laurence, and Atwood," *World Literature Written in English*, 20, 1 (Spring 1981), 133; Donna Gerstenberger, "Conceptions Literary and Otherwise," *Novel*, 9, 2 (Winter 1976), 150; Roberta Rubenstein, "*Surfacing*," *Modern Fiction Studies*, 22, 3 (Autumn 1976), 398; Cheryl Stokes Rackowski, "Women by Women," diss., University of Connecticut, 1978, 72; Karla Smart Kadrmas, "Owen Barfield Reads Margaret Atwood," in *Margaret Atwood*, ed. Beatrice Mendez-Egle (Edinburg, TX: Pan American University Press, 1987), 76.

14. See Francine du Plessix Gray, "Margaret Atwood," in her *Adam and Eve and the City* (New York: Simon and Schuster, 1987), 293; Evelyn J. Hinz, "The Religious Roots of the Feminine Identity Issue," in *Margaret Laurence*, ed. Christl Verduyn (Peterborough, ON: Broadview, 1988), 93; Carol P. Christ, who also mentions the narrator's concern with power, in her *Diving Deep and Surfacing* (Boston: Beacon, 1980), 41; Annis Pratt, "Surfacing and the Rebirth Journey," in *The Art of Margaret Atwood*, ed. Arnold E. Davidson and Cathy N. Davidson, 151; Lorraine Weir, "Atwood in a Landscape," in *Margaret*

Atwood, ed. Sherrill E. Grace and Lorraine Weir, 150; Rachel Blau DuPlessis, *Writing Beyond the Ending* (Bloomington, IN: Indiana University Press, 1985), 98; Jerome H. Rosenberg, *Margaret Atwood* (Boston: Twayne, 1984), 111; Lorelei Cederstrom, "The Regeneration of Time in Atwood's *Surfacing*," *Atlantis*, 6, 2 (Spring 1981), 35; John Moss, *Sex and Violence in the Canadian Novel* (Toronto: McClelland and Stewart, 1977), 139; Catherine Sheldrick Ross, "A Singing Spirit," *Atlantis*, 4, 1 (Fall 1978), 92; William C. James, "Atwood's Surfacing," *Canadian Literature*, 91 (Winter 1981), 176. Jane Rule argues that the novel fails at its own transformative project, "Life, Liberty and the Pursuit of Normalcy," *The Malahat Review*, 41 (January 1977), 46; Philip Kokotailo reviews criticism to distinguish between who reads the transformations as successful and who does not, "Form in Atwood's *Surfacing*," *Studies in Canadian Literature*, 8, 2 (1983), 155-165.

15. For literary approaches that treat the narrator's and/or Atwood's relationship with language, see Margaret Homans, "'Her Very Own Howl,'" *Signs*, 9, 2 (1983), 205; Nancy E. Bjerring, "The Problem of Language in Margaret Atwood's *Surfacing*," *Queen's Quarterly*, 83, 4 (Winter 1976), 600; Carolyn Allen, "Failures of Word, Uses of Silence," *Regionalism and the Female Imagination*, 4, 1 (Spring 1978), 6; Heather Murray, "The Synthetic Habit of Mind," *World Literature Written in English*, 25, 1 (1985), 102; Meera T. Clark, "Margaret Atwood's *Surfacing*," *Modern Poetry Studies*, 13, 3 (Summer 1983), 12; Catherine Rainwater, "The Sense of the Flesh in Four Novels by Margaret Atwood," in *Margaret Atwood*, ed. Beatrice Mendez-Egle, 21; Margaret Griffith, "Verbal Terrain in the Novels of Margaret Atwood," *Critique*, 21, 3 (1980), 90. Rosemary Sullivan differs from the other language critics in arguing that "Atwood's language fails her," "Breaking the Circle," *The Malahat Review*, 41 (January 1977), 40; Carole Gerson, "Margaret Atwood and Québec," *Studies in Canadian Literature*, 1,1(1976), 115-119.

For critics attending to literary form, genre, and allusion in the novel, see Donald R. Bartlett, "'Fact' and Form in *Surfacing*," *The University of Windsor Review*, 17, 1 (Fall-Winter 1982), 21; Robert Cluett, "Surface Structures," in *Margaret Atwood*, ed. Sherrill E. Grace and Lorraine Weir, 87; Philip Stratford, "The Uses of Ambiguity," in *Margaret Atwood*, ed. Sherrill E.Grace and Lorraine Weir, 115; Evelyn J. Hinz and John J. Teunissen, "*Surfacing*," *Contemporary Literature*, 20, 2 (Spring 1979), 229; Rosemary Sweetapple, "Margaret Atwood," *Southern Review* [Adelaide], 9, 1 (1976), 67; Sherrill E. Grace, *Violent Duality* (Montreal: Véhicule, 1980), 98; Adrienne Rich, *Of Woman Born* (New York: W.W. Norton, 1976), 240; Rosemary Sullivan, "Surfacing and Deliverance," *Canadian Literature*, 67 (Winter 1976), 17; Evelyn J. Hinz, "The Masculine/Feminine Psychology of American/Canadian

Primitivism," in *Other Voices, Other Views*, ed. Robin W. Winks (Westport, CT: Greenwood, 1978), p. 96; Marie-Françoise Guédon, "*Surfacing*," in *Margaret Atwood*, ed. Sherrill E. Grace and Lorraine Weir, 92; Theresia Quigley, "*Surfacing*," *The Antigonish Review*, 34 (Summer 1978), 84-85; Mara E. Donaldson, "Woman as Hero in Margaret Atwood's *Surfacing* and Maxine Hong Kingston's *The Woman Warrior*," in *Heroines of Popular Culture*, ed. Ray Browne (Bowling Green, OH: Bowling Green State University Popular Press, 1987), 102; Sue Thomas, "Mythic Reconception and the Mother/Daughter Relationship in Margaret Atwood's *Surfacing*," *Ariel*, 19, 2 (1988), 73; Charles Berryman, "Atwood's Narrative Quest," *The Journal of Narrative Technique*, 17, 1 (1987), 51-56; Manfred Mackenzie, "'I am a place,'" in *A Sense of Place in the New Literatures* in English, ed. Peggy Nightingale (St. Lucia: University of Queensland Press, 1986), 32-36.

For critics treating Atwood's relationship with writing as art, see Frank Davey, *Margaret Atwood* (Vancouver: Talonbooks, 1984), 63, and his "Atwood Walking Backwards," *Open Letter*. Second series, 5 (Summer 1973), 78; Kathryn VanSpanckeren, "Magic in the Novels of Margaret Atwood," in *Margaret Atwood*, ed. Beatrice Mendez-Egle, 11; Anne G. Jones, "Margaret Atwood," *The Hollins Critic*, 16, 3 (June 1979), 12.

16. Sally Robinson, "The 'Anti-Logos Weapon,'" *Contemporary Literature*, 29, 1 (1988), 111. An essay by George Bowering also refers to Kristevan theory, "Desire and the Unnamed Narrator," *Descant*, 19, 3 (1988), 19.

17. *Surfacing* (New York: Fawcett, 1972), 12. Other references to the novel will be cited in the text.

18. In response to Elizabeth Meese's statement that "*Surfacing* ... seems to be preoccupied with the father, but it really is also preoccupied with the mother," Atwood states that "the image in that book for the mother and the father is that little barometer that has the two figures of equal size balanced," "An Interview with Margaret Atwood," *Black Warrior Review*, 12, 1 (Fall 1985), 108.

19. Charlotte Walker Mendez compares early and late bird calls in the novel in connection with the narrator's learning of nature's language, "Loon Voice," in *Margaret Atwood*, ed. Beatrice Mendez-Egle, 89-94.

20. Interestingly, male and female critics differ in evaluating the narrator's mother's legacy: Peter Klovan writes that "[t]he mother's lasting influence on the narrator is probably quite devastating ... a model of profound helplessness," "'They Are Out of Reach Now,'" *Essays on Canadian Writing*, 33 (Fall 1986), 11; Lorna Irvine, on the other hand, in her reading of mother-daughter

relations in English-Canadian fiction links women writers' journeys back to mother with "a profoundly Canadian quest for a kingdom where hostility can be transformed peacefully to a unifying reconciliation," thereby giving the same broadly positive value to the narrator's memory of her mother that I do, "A Psychological Journey," in *The Lost Tradition*, ed. Cathy N. Davidson and E. M. Broner (New York: Ungar, 1980), 251; and Susan Fromberg Schaeffer argues that the mother's crucial lesson stresses the inevitability of loss in human experience, "'It Is Time That Separates Us,'" *The Centennial Review*, 18, 4 (Fall 1974), 337.

21. "Margaret Atwood," in *Eleven Canadian Novelists Interviewed by Graeme Gibson* (see note 3 above).

22. Of the narrator's rescuer, Margot Northey writes perceptively that "Joe and the people in the city are not yet Americans. Canadian society, like the individuals who comprise it, is only half formed and therefore still able to be shaped," *The Haunted Wilderness* (Toronto: University of Toronto Press, 1976), 69.

CHAPTER THREE

1. Joyce Carol Oates, "Margaret Atwood: Poems and Poet," *The New York Times Book Review*, 21 May 1978, 14. In a 1975 interview Atwood enlarges upon her interest in women's interrelationships with oblique reference as well to *Lady Oracle* in one of whose climactic scenes a maze appears: "[r]ight now I'm working with labyrinths. Labyrinths are very interesting. They were in fact a female religion. What you were supposed to find originally at the centre of the labyrinth was the Mother," in Gail Van Varseveld, "Talking with Atwood," *Room of One's Own*, I, 2 (1975), 68.

2. Elsa Cathrine Martens, "Interview with Margaret Atwood; Oslo, February 1979," in her "Mother and Daughter Relationships — A Growing Theme in the Writings of Margaret Atwood," M.A. Thesis, The University of Oslo [Norway], 1980, 115. This manuscript is housed among the Atwood Papers at the Thomas Fisher Rare Book Library, University of Toronto.

3. See Roberta Rubenstein, *Boundaries of the Self* (Urbana, IL: University of Illinois Press, 1987), 235; Sherrill E.Grace, *Violent Duality* (Montreal: Véhicule Press, 1980), 112-124; Frank Davey, *Margaret Atwood* (Vancouver: Talonbooks, 1984), 67; Roberta Sciff-Zamaro, "The Re/membering of the Female Power in *Lady Oracle*," *Canadian Literature*, 112 (Spring 1987), 32-

38; Barbara Godard, "My (m)Other, My Self," *Essays on Canadian Writing*, 26 (Summer 1983), 13-44; Sharon R.Wilson, "The Fragmented Self in *Lady Oracle*," *Commonwealth Novel in English*, 1, 1 (January 1982), 50-85; Molly Hite, "Other Side, Other Woman," in her *The Other Side of the Story* (Ithaca: Cornell, 1989), 127-167. Gayle Greene's reading seems closest to mine, arguing that Joan's matrophobia denies her "the maternal legacy that might empower her," in her *Changing the Story* (Bloomington, IN: Indiana University Press, 1991), 176.

4. See Francis Mansbridge, "Search for Self in the Novels of Margaret Atwood," *Journal of Canadian Fiction*, 22 (1978), 106-117; Lucy M. Freibert, "The Artist as Picaro," *Canadian Literature*, 92 (Spring 1982), 23-33; Catherine Sheldrick Ross, "'Banished To This Other Place,'" *English Studies in Canada*, 6, 4 (Winter 1980), 460-474; Russell M. Brown, "Atwood's Sacred Wells," *Essays on Canadian Writing*, 17 (Spring 1980), 5-43; Jessie Givner, "Mirror Images in Margaret Atwood's *Lady Oracle*," *Studies in Canadian Literature*, 41, 1 (1989), 141.

5. See Walter Wayne Fraser, "The Dominion of Women," diss., University of Manitoba, 1985, 344-360; Wilfred Cude, "The Female Quixote as Junkie," in his *A Due Sense of Differences* (Washington, DC: University Press of America, 1980), 133-153.

6. See Catherine Rainwater, "The Sense of the Flesh in Four Novels by Margaret Atwood," in *Maragaret Atwood*, ed. Beatrice Mendez-Egle (Edinburg, TX: Pan American University Press, 1987), 14-28; Carol L. Beran, "'At least its voice isn't mine': The Concept of Voice in Margaret Atwood's *Lady Oracle*," *Weber Studies*, 8, 1 (Spring 1991), 54-71.

7. See Cheryl Stokes Rackowski, "Women by Women," diss., University of Connecticut, 1978, 58. Rackowski refers specifically to "Arthur's narcissism" here but does not develop the observation.

8. J.R. (Tim) Struthers, "An Interview with Margaret Atwood," *Essays on Canadian Writing*, 6 (Spring 1977), 19. For my understanding of the typical Gothic plot I rely on Claire Kahane's summary:

> if the older Gothic tradition involved an obscure exploration of female identity through a confrontation with a diffuse spectral mother, in modern Gothic the spectral mother typically becomes an embodied actual figure. She, and not some threatening villain, becomes the primary antagonist. ("The Gothic Mirror," in *The (M)other Tongue*, ed. Shirley Nelson Garner et al., Ithaca, NY: Cornell University Press, 1985, 343)

Generic studies of the novel include Susan J. Rosowski on the gothic theme, "Margaret Atwood's *Lady Oracle*," *Research Studies*, 49, 2 (June 1981), 87-98; and Emily Jensen, "Margaret Atwood's *Lady Oracle*," *Essays on Canadian Writing*, 33 (Fall 1986), 29-49; Nora Foster Stovel, "Reflections on Mirror Images," *Essays on Canadian Writing*, 33 (Fall 1986), 50-67; Kathryn VanSpanckeren, "Magic in the Novels of Margaret Atwood," in *Margaret Atwood*, ed. Beatrice Mendez-Egle, 1-13; Robert Lecker, "Janus through the Looking Glass" and Clara Thomas, "*Lady Oracle*," in *The Art of Margaret Atwood*, ed. Arnold E. Davidson and Cathy N. Davidson (Toronto: Anansi, 1981) 159,178; Susan Jaret McKinstry, "Living Literally by the Pen," in *Margaret Atwood*, ed. Beatrice Mendez-Egle, 58-70; Jane Rule, "Life, Liberty and the Pursuit of Normalcy," *The Malahat Review*, 41 (January 1977) 42-49; Frank Davey, "*Lady Oracle*'s Secret," *Studies in Canadian Literature* (Fall 1980), 209-221; Sybil Korff Vincent, "The Mirror and the Cameo," in *The Female Gothic*, ed. Juliann E. Fleenor (Montreal: Eden Press, 1983), 153-163; Carol L. Beran, "George, Leda, and a Poured Concrete Balcony," *Canadian Literature*, 112 (Spring 1987), 18-28; Eleonora Rao, "Margaret Atwood's Lady Oracle," *British Journal of Canadian Studies*, 4, 1 (1989), 136-156.

9. *Lady Oracle* (Toronto: McClelland and Stewart, 1976), 228. Other references to the novel will be cited in the text.

10. Lawrence Martin, *Pledge of Allegiance* (Toronto: McClelland and Stewart, 1993), 36.

11. "A Conversation with Margaret Atwood," in *Margaret Atwood*, ed. Beatrice Mendez-Egle, 176.

12. "A Conversation with Margaret Atwood," 175.

13. Julia Kristeva, *Desire in Language*, ed. Leon S. Roudiez, trans. Thomas Gora et al. (New York: Columbia University Press, 1980), 140.

14. Margaret Atwood, "A Disneyland of the Soul," in *The Writer and Human Rights*, ed. Toronto Arts Group for Human Rights (New York: Anchor, 1983), 130, 129, 131, 132. (The previous three quotations are from this text, as I have just noted in the page numbers cited.)

15. Lorna Irvine cites the volume as the first in which Atwood "has created a dominantly female world" where she "celebrates women," "One Woman Leads to Another," in *The Art of Margaret Atwood*, ed. Arnold E. Davidson and Cathy N. Davidson, 95, 105. Sherrill E. Grace argues that it is, "to date, the volume which most deliberately celebrates natural processes, connections, and continuities," "Articulating the 'Space Between,'" in *Margaret Atwood*, ed. Sherrill

E. Grace and Lorraine Weir (Vancouver: University of British Columbia Press, 1983), 13; elsewhere Grace reads the title sequence as treatment of the French-English Canadian question, "Margaret Atwood and the Poetics of Duplicity," in *The Art of Margaret Atwood*, ed. Arnold E. Davidson and Cathy N. Davidson, 66-68. Frank Davey reads it as evidence of the confluence of two recurrent themes in Atwood's writing, "feminism and ecology," and as an extension of her critique of interpersonal power politics to those international, in his *Margaret Atwood* (Vancouver: Talonbooks, 1984), 29.

16. George Woodcock writes, "I do not think there is any book by Atwood that is more tender in its tone," in *Margaret Atwood*, ed. Sherrill E. Grace and Lorraine Weir, 134. Jerome H. Rosenberg calls "a major dynamic" of this work its "hope," in his *Margaret Atwood* (Boston: Twayne, 1984), 84. Judith McCombs writes that the volume represents Atwood's speakers' movement from a "Closed, Divided, Mirroring World" to "the realistic Open World," "Atwood's fictive portraits of the artist," *Women's Studies*, 12 (1986), 69.

17. Sandra Henneberger, "Strange and Playful Paradigms in Margaret Atwood's Poetry," *Women's Studies*, 17 (1990), 279.

18. Luce Irigaray, "And the One Doesn't Stir without the Other," trans. Hélène Vivienne Wenzel, *Signs*, 7, 1 (1981), 61-62.

19. Kristeva, *Tales of Love*, trans. Leon S. Roudiez (New York: Columbia, 1987), 26.

20. *Two-Headed Poems* (New York; Simon and Schuster, 1978), 67. Other references to this work will be cited in the text.

21. General studies of Atwood's poetry that either bear directly on my interpretation or are simply distinctive are: Lorna Irvine's, arguing that "[w]hat history has separated — the image of male and female — the poet attempts to join," "The Red and Silver Heroes Have Collapsed," *Concerning Poetry*, 12, 2 (1979), 64; and Katherine E. Waters' linking sexual politics with imperialism and proposing an alternative "'female perspective'" which is both "more appalling than the 'male' one" and "more potentially creative" in its "chaos of non-perspective, of subject-object confusion, of loss of ego-self," "Margaret Atwood," in MOTHER *was not a person*, ed. Margret Andersen, 102, 112; Sandra Djwa situates Atwood in a tradition of Canadian poetry privileging "devolution," "The Where of Here," in *The Art of Margaret Atwood*, ed. Arnold E. Davidson and Cathy N. Davidson, 34; and John Wilson Foster states further, with reference to Atwood's study of native Canadian mythology, that "[b]ecause the Canadian landscape is so various and primitive, and

not cultivated to a European degree, it facilitates man's awareness of the pri-
mordial," "The Poetry of Margaret Atwood," *Canadian Literature*, 74
(Autumn 1977), 15; D. G. Jones shows not Frye's but McLuhan's possible
influence on Atwood, writing that McLuhan's prediction of a revolt in repre-
sentational art against "the hegemony of the eye" in fact becomes a "denigra-
tion of the eye — above all the camera eye — evident in the imagery of Page,
Avison, and Atwood," "Cold Eye and Optic Heart," *Modern Poetry Studies*, 5,
2 (Autumn 1974), 172, 185; Russell M. Brown names "mass culture" as
Atwood's target while suggesting that "like many mystics," Atwood "does not
want to renounce the world but rather to draw us more deeply into it,"
including presumably popular culture, "Atwood's Sacred Wells," *Essays on
Canadian Writing*, 17 (Spring 1980), 22, 41. Sherrill E. Grace alone sees a
connection between Atwood's work and Kristeva's theory of poetic language,
although Grace does not pursue the connection at any length: "shattering the
constraints of rationalist discourse in order to release the rhythms and emotions of a semiotic process, she articulates the space ... between," "Articulating
the 'Space Between,'" in *Margaret Atwood*, ed. Sherrill E. Grace and Lorraine
Weir, 12. Cheryl Walker demonstrates Atwood's affinity with deconstruction
while noting that in *Two-Headed Poems*, "the Modernist hunger makes its way
back ... by way of a call to faith," "Turning to Margaret Atwood," in *Margaret
Atwood*, ed. Beatrice Mendez-Egle, 166.

CHAPTER FOUR

1. Jo Brans, "Using What You're Given," *Southwest Review*, 68, 4, 303.

2. Elaine Tuttle Hansen in the only generic treatment of the novel shows Rennie
    as deconstructive in her thinking and places the text in the tradition of "femi-
    nist and late twentieth-century fictions" which "reject old illusions of consen-
    sus and community," "Fiction and (Post) Feminism in Atwood's *Bodily
    Harm*," *Novel: A Forum on Fiction*, 19, 1 (Fall 1985), 18, 20.

3. Jennifer Waelti-Walters calls the novel "a piece of overt misogyny," "Double-
    Read," *Room of One's Own*, 8, 4 (1984), 121. Jerome Rosenberg argues for
    Atwood's "pessimism" and Rennie's refusal to accept her power with words, in
    his *Margaret Atwood* (Boston: Twayne, 1984), 133, 130. Frank Davey notes
    Rennie's "passivity" and entrapment in "the static patterns of [her] art," in his
    Margaret Atwood (Vancouver: Talonbooks, 1984), 64, 63. Stanley S. Atherton
    claims that Rennie remains unwilling to see past her stereotypes of the
    Caribbean to understand it clearly, in his "Atwood, Horwood, Kreiner and

Wright: The Caribbean Connection," in *Tensions between North and South*, ed. Edith Mettke (Wurzburg: Konigshausen and Neumann, 1990), 36.

4. Catherine Rainwater writes that for Rennie "the discovery or assertion of physical power coincides with the experience of linguistic power," "The Sense of the Flesh in Four Novels by Margaret Atwood," 24; and Mary K. Kirtz defends Rennie's transformation for what it teaches, the "third thing" in Atwood's thinking between "detachment" and "despair," "The Thematic Imperative," 127, both in *Margaret Atwood* (Edinburg, TX: Pan American University Press, 1987). Nora Foster Stovel observes that Rennie avoids mirrors because of her own "bodily harm" but learns to accept and face death by facing Lora, "Reflections on Mirror Images," *Essays on Canadian Writing*, 33 (Fall 1986), 64, 66. Diana Brydon claims that Rennie as an "unsympathetic" character "forces her readers to think as well as feel," "Caribbean Revolution and Literary Convention," *Canadian Literature*, 95 (Winter 1982), 184. Coral Ann Howells views Atwood as succesfully "attempting to revise the categories of 'Canadian' and 'female,'" in her *Private and Fictional Words* (London: Methuen, 1987), 54; Denise E. Lynch writes that Atwood's plot "enacts a process of ... restructuring a unified self in dynamic relation to the community," "Personalist Plot in Atwood's *Bodily Harm*," *Studies in the Humanities*, 15, 1 (1988), 46; Jean Wyatt states that by regaining her ability to connect with others Rennie frees her own creativity, previously guarded and blocked by emotional detachment, in her *Reconstructing Desire* (Chapel Hill, NC: University of North Carolina Press, 1990), 114-115.

5. *Bodily Harm* (New York: Bantam, 1983), 30. Other references to this work are cited in the text.

6. Charles Taylor, *The Malaise of Modernity* (Toronto: Anansi, 1991), 9.

7. Catharine R. Stimpson writes that in this study of "the appetite for domination" Atwood "links the morality of the Aunt to that of radical feminists. The Aunts are repressive. Radical feminists can be repressive too," "Atwood Woman," *The Nation*, 31 May 1986, 766, 765. Gayle Greene argues that "Gilead has happened partly because of the failure of feminism to effect social change," women's failure given increased freedoms "to imagine more various shapes for our lives," "Choice of Evils," *The Women's Review of Books*, 3, 10 (July 1986), 14, 15. Coral Ann Howells states in a thematic interpretation closest to mine that "[w]hat the Aunts' tyranny demonstrates is the danger that patriarchal authority may merely be delegated to become matriarchal authority if the psychology of power politics with its traditional patterns of domination and submission remains unchanged," in her *Private and Fictional Words*, 65. See also Deborah Silverton Rosenfelt, "Feminism, 'Postfeminism,'

and Contemporary Women's Fiction," in *Traditions and the Talents of Women*, ed. Florence Howe (Urbana, IL: University of Illinois Press, 1991), 282-283.

8. David Ketterer, "Margaret Atwood's *The Handmaid's Tale*," *Science-Fiction Studies* #48, 16 (1989), 209-217; Patrick D. Murphy, "Reducing the Dystopian Distance," *Science-Fiction Studies* #52, 17 (1990), 25-40; Kingsley Widmer, "Antifemtopian Feminism and Atwood," in his *Counterings* (Ann Arbor, MI: University of Michigan Research Press, 1988), 75-80; Frances Bartkowski, "No Shadows without Light," in her *Feminist Utopias* (Lincoln, NB: University of Nebraska, 1989), 133-158; Amin Malak, "Margaret Atwood's *The Handmaid's Tale* and the Dystopian Tradition," *Canadian Literature*, 112 (1987), 9-16; Roberta Rubenstein, "Nature and Nurture in Dystopia," in *Margaret Atwood*, ed. Kathryn VanSpanckeren and Jan Garden Castro (Carbondale, IL: Southern Illinois University Press, 1989), 101-112; Reingard M. Nischik, "Back to the Future," *Englisch-Amerikanische Studien*, 5, 1 (1987), 139-148; Glenn Deer, "Rhetorical Strategies in *The Handmaid's Tale*," *English Studies in Canada*, 18, 2 (June 1992), 215-233; Peter Fitting, "Recent Feminist Utopias," in *Mindscapes*, ed. George E. Slusser and Eric S. Rabkin (Carbondale, IL: Southern Illinois University Press, 1989), 156-157; Chris Ferns, "The Value/s of Dystopia," *Dalhousie Review*, 69, 3 (Fall 1989), 373-382.

9. Linda Kaufmann, "Special Delivery," in *Writing the Female Voice*, ed. Elizabeth C. Goldsmith (Boston: Northeastern University Press, 1989), 221-244; W.J. Keith, "Apocalyptic Imaginations," *Essays on Canadian Writing*, 35 (1987), 123-134; Madonne Miner, "'Trust Me [treatment of romance],'" *Twentieth Century Literature*, 37, 2 (Summer 1991), 148-168; Stephanie Barbé Hammer, "The World As It Will Be? [treatment of satire]," *Modern Language Studies*, 20, 2 (Spring 1990), 39-49.

10. Harriet F. Bergmann, "Teaching Them to Read," *College English*, 51, 8 (1989), 847-854; W.F. Garrett-Petts, "Reading, Writing, and the Postmodern Condition," *Open Letter*. Seventh Series, 1 (1988), 74-92; Ken Norris, "'The University of Denay, Nunavit,'" *American Review of Canadian Studies* (Autumn 1990), 357-364.

11. Michele Lacombe, "The Writing on the Wall," *Wascana Review*, 21, 2 (1986), 3-20.

12. David Cowart, "The Way It Will Be," in his *History and the Contemporary Novel* (Carbondale, IL: Southern Illinois University Press, 1989), 105-119; Arnold E. Davidson, "Future Tense," in *Margaret Atwood*, ed. Kathryn

VanSpanckeren and Jan Garden Castro (Carbondale, IL: Southern Illinois University Press, 1988), 113-121.

13. Chinmoy Banerjee, "Alice in Disneyland," *Essays on Canadian Writing*, 41 (1990), 74-92; Paul Hjartarson, "The Literary Canon and Its Discontent," in *Literatures in Canada/Littératures au Canada*, ed. Deborah C. Poff, 10, 5 (Ottawa: Association for Canadian Studies and International Council for Canadian Studies, 1988), 67-80.

14. *The Handmaid's Tale* (Toronto: McClelland and Stewart, 1985), 132. Other references to this work are cited in the text.

CHAPTER FIVE

1. Margaret Atwood, "Canadian-American Relations," *Second Words* (Boston: Beacon, 1984), 381.

2. My first reference to *Interlunar* (Toronto: Oxford, 1984) is to p. 29; others are cited in the text.

3. Julia Kristeva, *Black Sun*, trans. Leon S. Roudiez (New York: Columbia University Press, 1989), 14.

4. *Cat's Eye* (Toronto: McClelland and Stewart, 1988). Other references to this novel will be cited in the text.

5. See for example: Douglas Glover, "Her life entire," review essay, *Books in Canada* (October 1988), 11-14; Judith Timson, "Atwood's Triumph," *Maclean's*, 3 October 1988, 56-58, 60-61; Robert Fulford, "Kernel of glass at the heart of new Atwood heroine," *Quill and Quire* (October 1988), 18; Alberto Manguel, "First Impressions," *Saturday Night* (November 1988), 67-68, 70; "A Rich Talent for all Seasons," *Maclean's*, 26 December 1988, 35; Caryn James, "Ambiguity Between Best Girlfriends," *The New York Times*, late ed., 28 January 1989, 16; Shena Mackay, "The painter's revenges," *Times Literary Supplement*, 3-9 February 1989, 113; Alice McDermott, "What Little Girls Are Really Made of," *The New York Times Book Review*, 5 February 1989, 1, 35; Stefan Kanfer, "Time Arrested," *Time*, Canadian ed., 6 February 1989, 66; Alison Lurie, "The Mean Years," *Ms.* (March 1989), 38, 41; Hermione Lee, "Little Women," *The New Republic*, 10 April 1989, 38-40; Helen Yglesias, "Odd Woman Out," *The Women's Review of Books*, 6,10-11, July 1989, 3-4; Chinmoy Banerjee, "Atwood's Time," *Modern Fiction Studies*, 36, 4 (Winter 1990), 513-522.

6. Judith McCombs, "Contrary Re-memberings," *Canadian Literature*, 129 (1991), 9-23.

7. Jessie Givner, "Names, Faces and Signatures in Margaret Atwood's *Cat's Eye* and *The Handmaid's Tale*," *Canadian Literature*, 133 (Summer 1992), 56-75.

8. Sherrill E. Grace, "Surviving with Atwood," *The Canadian Forum*, November 1991, 30-33.

9. Aamer Hussein, "Strategies for survival," *Times Literary Supplement*, 13 September 1991, 20; John Bemrose, "Studies in suffering," *Maclean's*, 16 September 1991, 58; Daniel Jones, "Atwood's Dark Parables, Davies's Ballad of Bankruptcy," *Quill and Quire* (August 1991), 14.

10. Margaret Atwood, *Wilderness Tips* (Toronto: McClelland and Stewart, 1991), 44. Other references to this novel will be cited in the text.

11. Margaret Atwood, *Survival* (Toronto: Anansi, 1972), 38-39.

12. James Wilcox, "The Hairball on the Mantelpiece," *The New York Times Book Review*, 24 November 1991, 7.

CONCLUSION

1. Rick Salutin, "The future of our past," *Books in Canada* (January-February 1988), 11.

2. Margaret Atwood, *If You Love This Country* (Toronto: McClelland and Stewart, 1987), 23.

3. Margaret Atwood, *Cat's Eye* (Toronto: McClelland and Stewart, 1988), 87.

4. Margaret Atwood, *Wilderness Tips* (Toronto: McClelland and Stewart, 1991), 187-188.

5. Marilyn French, *Beyond Power* (New York: Summit, 1985), 443.

6. Margaret Atwood, *The Handmaid's Tale* (Toronto: McClelland and Stewart, 1985), 139.

7. Julia Kristeva, *Nations Without Nationalism*, trans. Leon S. Roudiez (New York: Columbia University Press, 1993), 35.

WORKS CONSULTED

PRIMARY SOURCES

FICTION

Atwood, Margaret. *Bluebeard's Egg*. Toronto: McClelland and Stewart, 1983.

———. *Bodily Harm*. Toronto: McClelland and Stewart, 1981

———. *Cat's Eye*. Toronto: McClelland and Stewart, 1988.

———. *Dancing Girls and Other Stories*. Toronto: McClelland and Stewart, 1977.

———. *The Edible Woman*. Toronto: McClelland and Stewart, 1969.

———. *Good Bones*. Toronto: Coach House Press, 1992.

———. *The Handmaid's Tale*. Toronto: McClelland and Stewart, 1985.

———. *Lady Oracle*. Toronto: McClelland and Stewart, 1976.

———. *Life Before Man*. Toronto: McClelland and Stewart, 1979.

———. *Surfacing*. Toronto: McClelland and Stewart, 1972.

———. *Wilderness Tips*. Toronto: McClelland and Stewart, 1991.

POETRY

———. *The Animals in That Country*. Toronto: Oxford University Press, 1968.

———. *The Circle Game*. Toronto: Anansi, 1966.

———. *Interlunar*. Toronto: Oxford University Press, 1984.

———. *The Journals of Susanna Moodie*. Toronto: Oxford University Press, 1970.

———. *Murder in the Dark*. Toronto: Coach House Press, 1983.

———. ed. *The New Oxford Book of Canadian Verse in English*. Toronto: Oxford University Press, 1982.

———. *Power Politics*. Toronto: Anansi, 1971.

———. *Procedures for Underground*. Boston: Little, Brown, 1970.

———. *Selected Poems II: Poems Selected and New 1976-1986*. Toronto: Oxford University Press, 1986.

———. *True Stories*. Toronto: Oxford University Press, 1981.

———. *Two-Headed Poems*. Toronto: Oxford University Press, 1978.

———. *You Are Happy*. Toronto: Oxford University Press, 1974.

CRITICISM

———. "A Disneyland of the Soul." In *The Writer and Human Rights*. Ed. Toronto Arts Group for Human Rights. 129-132. Toronto: Lester & Orpen Dennys, 1984

———. "Free traders don't eat quiche." *The Globe and Mail*, 17 November 1988. A7.

———. "Margaret Atwood [Acceptance Speech, 1987 Humanist of the Year]." *The Humanist* (September-October 1987): 5-8.

———. "Nature and Power in the English Metaphysical Romance of the Nineteenth and Twentieth Centuries." Unfinished diss., Harvard University, 1967.

———. "Notes on Power Politics." *Acta Victoriana* 97, 2 (1973): 7-19.

———. "A Reply." *Signs* 2, 2 (1976): 340-341.

———. *Second Words: Selected Critical Prose*. Toronto: House of Anansi, 1982

———. *Survival: A Thematic Guide to Canadian Literature*. Toronto: Anansi, 1972.

MEMOIRS

———. "Great Aunts." In *Family Portraits: Remembrances by Twenty Distinguished Writers*. Ed. Carolyn Anthony. 3-16. New York: Doubleday, 1989.

INTERVIEWS

"An *Atlantis* Interview with Margaret Atwood." *Atlantis* 5, 2 (1980): 202-211.

Brans, Jo. "Using What You're Given: An Interview with Margaret Atwood." *Southwest Review* 68, 4 (1983): 301-315.

Castro, Jan Garden. "Interview with Margaret Atwood." *River Styx* 15 (1984): 6-21.

Davidson, Jim. "Margaret Atwood." *Meanjin* 37, 2 (1978): 189-205.

Draine, Betsy. "An Interview with Margaret Atwood." In *Interviews with Contemporary Writers*. Second Series. Ed. L. S. Dembo. Madison, WI: University of Wisconsin Press, 1983.

Gibson, Graeme. "Margaret Atwood." In *Eleven Canadian Novelists Interviewed by Graeme Gibson*. Toronto: Anansi, 1973.

Hammond, Karla. "An Interview with Margaret Atwood." *The American Poetry Review* 8, 5 (1979): 27-29.

Ingersoll, Earl G., ed. *Margaret Atwood: Conversations*. Willowdale, ON: Firefly Books, 1990.

Kaminski, Margaret. "Interview with Margaret Atwood," *Waves* 4, 1 (1975): 8-13.

Langer, Beryl. "Taking issue: Interview with Margaret Atwood," *Australian-Canadian Studies* 6, 1 (1988): 125-136.

Living Author Series Interviewer. "A Conversation with Margaret Atwood." In *Margaret Atwood: Reflection and Reality*. Ed. Beatrice Mendez-Egle. Edinburg, TX: Pan American University Press, 1987.

Lyons, Bonnie. "An Interview with Margaret Atwood." *Shenandoah: The Washington and Lee University Review* 37, 2 (1987): 69-89.

"A Margaret Atwood Interview with Karla Hammond." *Concerning Poetry* 12, 2 (1979): 73-81.

Martens, Elsa Cathrine. "Interview with Margaret Atwood; Oslo, February 1979." In Martens's "Mother and Daughter Relationships — A Growing Theme in the Writings of Margaret Atwood." M.A. Thesis Oslo 1980. Margaret Atwood Papers. University of Toronto.

Meese, Elizabeth. "An Interview with Margaret Atwood." *Black Warrior Review* [The University of Alabama] 12, 1 (1985): 88-108.

Oates, Joyce Carol. "Margaret Atwood: Poems and Poet." *The New York Times Book Review*, 21 May 1978, 14, 43-45.

Sandler, Linda. "Interview with Margaret Atwood." *The Malahat Review* 41 (1977): 7-27.

Schreiber, Le Anne. "Female Trouble." *Vogue* (January 1986): 208-209.

Struthers, J. R. (Tim), "An Interview with Margaret Atwood." *Essays on Canadian Writing* 6 (1977): 18-27.

Van Varseveld, Gail. "Talking with Atwood." *Room of One's Own* 1, 2 (1975): 66-70.

SECONDARY SOURCES
GENERAL

Coward, Rosalind, and John Ellis. *Language and Materialism: Developments in Semiology and the Theory of the Subject.* London, UK: Routledge and Kegan Paul, 1977.

Gunew, Sneja. "Framing Marginality: Distinguishing the Textual Politics of the Marginal Voice." *Southern Review* [Adelaide] 18 (1985): 142-156.

—————, ed. *A Reader in Feminist Knowledge.* London, UK: Routledge, 1991.

Hill, Alette Olin. *Mother Tongue: Father Time: A Decade of Linguistic Revolt.* Bloomington, IN: Indiana University Press, 1986.

Hobsbawm, E. J. *Nations and Nationalism since 1780: Program, Myth, Reality.* 2nd edition. Cambridge, UK: Cambridge University Press, 1992.

LaPierre, Laurier, ed. *If You Love This Country: Facts and Feelings on Free Trade.* Toronto: McClelland and Stewart, 1987.

Parker, Andrew, et al., eds. *Nationalisms and Sexualities.* New York: Routledge, 1992.

George Steiner: A Reader. Ed. and Intro. George Steiner. Harmondsworth, UK: Penguin, 1984.

Taylor, Charles. *The Malaise of Modernity.* Toronto: Anansi, 1991.

CANADIAN LITERARY CRITICISM
AND THEORY (GENERAL)

Andersen, Margret. "Preface." In MOTHER was not a person. Ed. Margret Andersen. Montreal: Black Rose Books, 1972.

Berthoff, Robert J., ed. Credences [Proceedings of Festival of Canadian Poetry]new series 2, 2-3 (1983).

Bukoski, Anthony, "The Canadian Writer and the Iowa Experience." Canadian Literature 101 (1984): 15-34.

Cameron, Barry, and Michael Dixon. "Introduction, Mandatory Subversive Manifesto: Canadian Criticism vs. Literary Criticism," Studies in Canadian Literature 2, 2 (1977): 137-145.

Cappon, Paul. ed. In Our Own House: Social Perspectives on Canadian Literature. Toronto: McClelland and Stewart, 1978.

Cook, Eleanor, et al., eds. Centre and Labyrinth: Essays in Honour of Northrop Frye, Toronto: University of Toronto Press, 1983.

Cook, Ramsay. "Imagining a North American Garden: Some Parallels and Differences in Canadian and American Culture." Canadian Literature 103 (1984): 10-23.

Cude, Wilfred. A Due Sense of Differences: An Evaluative Approach to Canadian Literature. Washington, DC: University Press of America, 1980.

Davey, Frank. "A Response to Jean Mallinson's 'Poetry and Ideology.'" Studies in Canadian Literature 3, 2 (1978): 286-287.

———. From There to Here: A Guide to English-Canadian Literature since 1960. Erin, ON: Press Porcepic, 1974.

——— and bp Nichol, eds. "Robert Kroetsch: Essays." Open Letter. Fifth Series, 4 (1983).

Fee, Margery. "English-Canadian Literary Criticism, 1890-1950: Defining and Establishing a National Literature." Diss. University of Toronto, 1981.

Fraser, Walter Wayne. "The Dominion of Women: The Relationship of the Personal and the Political in Canadian Women's Literature." Diss. University of Manitoba, 1985.

Frye, Northrop. The Bush Garden: Essays on the Canadian Imagination. Toronto: Anansi, 1971.

————. "Conclusion." *Literary History of Canada*. Vol. III. Ed. Carl F. Klinck. Toronto: University of Toronto Press, 1976.

Grant, George. *Technology and Empire: Perspectives on North America*. Toronto: Anansi, 1969.

Howells, Coral Ann. *Private and Fictional Words: Canadian Women Novelists of the 1970s and 1980s*. London, UK: Methuen, 1987.

Irvine, Lorna. "A Psychological Journey: Mothers and Daughters in English-Canadian Fiction." In *The Lost Tradition: Mothers and Daughters in Literature*. Eds. Cathy N. Davidson and E. M. Broner. New York: Ungar, 1980.

Kroetsch, Robert, ed. "A Canadian Issue." *Boundary 2*, 3, 1 (1974).

————, and Reingard M. Nischik, eds. *Gaining Ground: European Critics on Canadian Literature*. Edmonton: NeWest, 1985.

Literary History of Canada: Canadian Literature in English. Volume 4. 2nd edition. Toronto: University of Toronto Press, 1990.

Mallinson, Jean. "Ideology and Poetry: An Examination of Some Recent Trends in Canadian Criticism," *Studies in Canadian Literature* 3, 1 (1978): 93-109.

Mandel, Eli, ed. *Contexts of Canadian Criticism*. Chicago, IL: University of Chicago Press, 1971.

Mansbridge, Francis. "Narcissism in the Modern Canadian Novel," *Studies in Canadian Literature* 6, 1 (1981): 232-244.

Moss, John, ed. *The Canadian Novel: Here and Now*. Toronto: New Canada Press, 1978.

————, ed. and intro. *Future Indicative: Literary Theory and Canadian Literature*. Ottawa: University of Ottawa Press, 1987.

————. *Sex and Violence in the Canadian Novel: The Ancestral Past*. Toronto: McClelland and Stewart, 1977.

Northey, Margot. *The Haunted Wilderness; The Gothic and Grotesque in Canadian Fiction*. Toronto: University of Toronto Press, 1976.

Rackowski, Cheryl Stokes, "Women by Women: Five Contemporary English and French Canadian Novelists," Ph. D. Diss. University of Connecticut 1978.

Salutin, Rick. "The future of our past." *Books in Canada* (January/February 1988): 7-11.

Sarkonak, Ralph, ed. "The Language of Difference: Writing in QUEBEC(ois)." *Yale French Studies* (1983): 65

Steven, Laurence. "Margaret Atwood's 'Polarities' and George Grant's Polemics." *American Review of Canadian Studies* 18, 4 (1988): 443-454.

Wilden, Tony. *The Imaginary Canadian.* Vancouver: Pulp Press, 1980.

Woodcock, George, ed. *The Canadian Novel in the Twentieth Century: Essays from Canadian Literature.* Toronto: McClelland and Stewart, 1975.

———. *The World of Canadian Writing: Critiques and Recollections.* Vancouver: Douglas and McIntyre, 1980.

CANADIAN HISTORY (GENERAL)

Bell, David, and Lorne Tepperman. *The Roots of Disunity: A Look at Canadian Political Culture.* Toronto: McClelland and Stewart, 1979.

Bothwell, Robert, Ian Drummond, and John English. *Canada Since 1945: Power, Politics, and Provincialism.* Toronto: University of Toronto Press, 1981.

Brown, Rosemary. "A New Kind of Power." In *Women in the Canadian Mosaic.* Ed. Gwen Matheson. Toronto: Peter Martin Associates, 1976.

Burns, John F., "A Leftist Leader Surging in Canada." *The New York Times,* Sunday edition, 8 November 1987, Sec. 1: 1, 8.

Christian, William. "Ideology and Politics in Canada." In *Approaches to Canadian Politics.* 2nd edition. Ed. John A. Redekop. Scarborough, ON: Prentice-Hall Canada, 1983.

Martin, Lawrence. *Pledge of Allegiance: The Americanization of Canada in the Mulroney Years.* Toronto: McClelland and Stewart, 1993.

McKillop, A. B. *Contours of Canadian Thought.* Toronto: University of Toronto Press, 1987.

McNaught, Kenneth. *The Pelican History of Canada.* Harmondsworth, UK: Penguin, 1983.

Newman, Peter C. "Bold and Cautious." In "Special Report: Portrait of Two Nations." *Maclean's* (3 July 1989): 23-84.

Nichols, Mark. "Canadians Speak Out on Issues and Hopes." *Maclean's* (4 January 1988): 34-37.

Penner, Norman. "The Development of Social Democracy in Canada." In *Political Thought in Canada: Contemporary Perspectives.* Ed. Stephen Brooks. Toronto: Irwin, 1984.

"The People's Verdict: How Canadians Can Agree on Their Future." *Maclean's* (1 July 1991): 10-76.

Thorburn, Hugh G., ed. "Section Four: Third Parties," In *Party Politics in Canada.* 5th edition. Scarborough, ON: Prentice-Hall Canada, 1985.

PSYCHOANALYTIC THEORY AND CRITICISM (GENERAL)

Adlam, Diana, and Couze Venn. "Introduction to Irigaray." *Ideology and Consciousness* 1 (1977): 57-61.

Barzilai, Shuli. "Borders of Language: Kristeva's Critique of Lacan." *PMLA* 106, 2 (March 1991): 294-305.

Benjamin, Jessica. "A Desire of One's Own: Psychoanalytic Feminism and Intersubjective Space." Working Paper No. 2, University of Wisconsin-Milwaukee: Center for Twentieth Century Studies, 1985. Report in *Feminist Studies/Critical Studies.* Ed. Teresa de Lauretis. Bloomington, IN: Indiana University Press, 1986.

Burke, Carolyn. "Introduction to Luce Irigaray's 'When Our Lips Speak Together.'" *Signs* 6, 1 (1980): 66-68.

———. "Report from Paris: Women's Writing and the Women's Movement." *Signs* 3, 4 (1978): 843-855.

"Christopher Lasch and Critics on the Family." *Tikkun* 1, 2 (1986): 85-97.

"Contemporary Feminist Thought in France: Translating Difference." In *The Future of Difference.* Eds. Hester Eisenstein and Alice Jardine, 71-121. Boston: G. K. Hall, 1980.

Critical Inquiry 8, 2 (Winter 1987), passim.

Diggins, John P., and Mark E. Kann, eds. *The Problem of Authority in America.* Philadelphia, PA: Temple University Press, 1981.

Ehrlich, Robert. "Review of *The Culture of Narcissism: American Life in an Age of Diminishing Expectations,* by Christopher Lasch." *Telos* 40 (1979): 187-198.

Freud, Sigmund. "Femininity," In Volume XXII of *The Standard Edition of the Complete Psychological Works.* Ed. James Strachey, 112-135. London, UK: Hogarth, [1953-1974] .

————. "On Narcissism," In Volume XIV of *The Standard Edition*, 67-102.

Garner, Shirley Nelson, Claire Kahane, and Madelon Sprengnether, eds. *The (M)other Tongue: Essays in Feminist Psychoanalytic Interpretation.* Ithaca, NY: Cornell University Press, 1985.

Gilligan, Carol. *In a Different Voice: Psychological Theory and Women's Development.* Cambridge, MA: Harvard University Press, 1982.

Gilman, Sander L., ed. *Introducing Psychoanalytic Theory.* New York: Brunner/Mazel, 1982.

Irigaray, Luce. "And the One Doesn't Stir without the Other." Trans. Hélène Vivienne Wenzel. *Signs* 7, 1 (1981): 60-67.

————. *Speculum of the Other Woman.* Trans. Gillian C. Gill. Ithaca, NY: Cornell University Press, 1985.

————. "Women's Exile." Trans. Couze Venn. *Ideology and Consciousness* 1 (May 1977): 62-76.

————."When Our Lips Speak Together." Trans. Carolyn Burke, *Signs* 6, 1 (1980): 69-79.

Jardine, Alice. "Introduction to Julia Kristeva's 'Women's Time.'" *Signs* 7, 1 (1981): 5-12.

Kernberg, Otto F. *Borderline Conditions and Pathological Narcissism.* New York: Jason Aronson, 1975.

Kohut, Heinz. *The Analysis of the Self.* New York: International Universities Press, 1971.

Kristeva, Julia. *Black Sun: Depression and Melancholia.* Trans. Leon S. Roudiez. New York: Columbia University Press, 1989.

————. *Desire in Language: A Semiotic Approach to Literature and Art.* Trans. Thomas Gora, Alice Jardine, and Leon S. Roudiez. New York: Columbia University Press, 1980.

————. *Language: The Unknown: An Initiation into Linguistics.* Trans. Anne M. Menke. New York: Columbia University Press, 1989.

————. "The Maternal Body." Trans. Claire Pajaczkowska. *m/f* 5-6 (1981): 158-163.

————. *Nations Without Nationalism.* Trans. Leon S. Roudiez. New York: Columbia University Press, 1993.

————. *Powers of Horror: An Essay on Abjection.* Trans. Leon S. Roudiez. New York: Columbia University Press, 1982.

————. *Revolution in Poetic Language.* Trans. Margaret Waller. New York: Columbia University Press, 1984.

————. "Stabat Mater." Trans. Arthur Goldhammer. In *The Female Body in Western Culture: Contemporary Perspectives.* Ed. Susan Rubin Suleiman. Cambridge, MA: Harvard University Press, 1986. Also in Kristeva's *Histoires d'amour.* Paris: Denoël, 1983.

————. *Strangers to Ourselves.* Trans. Leon S. Roudiez. New York: Columbia University Press, 1991.

————. *Tales of Love.* Trans. Leon S. Roudiez. New York: Columbia University Press, 1987.

————. "Women's Time." Trans. Alice Jardine and Harry Blake. *Signs* 7, 1 (1981): 13-35.

Lacan, Jacques. *Ecrits: A Selection.* Trans. Alan Sheridan. New York: W. W. Norton, 1977.

LaCapra, Dominick. "History and Psychoanalysis," Occasional Paper No. 5. University of Minnesota: Center for Humanistic Studies, 1985.

Lasch, Christopher. *The Culture of Narcissism: American Life in an Age of Diminishing Expectations.* New York: W. W. Norton, 1978.

————. *Haven in a Heartless World: The Family Besieged.* New York: Basic Books, 1977.

————. *The Minimal Self: Psychic Survival in Troubled Times.* New York: W. W. Norton, 1984.

————. "What's Wrong with the Right." *Tikkun* 1, 1 (1986): 23-29.

Lechte, John. *Julia Kristeva.* London, UK: Routledge, 1990.

Marks, Elaine. "Women and Literature in France." *Signs* 3, 4 (1978): 832-842.

Moi, Toril. "French Feminist Theory." In *Sexual/Textual Politics*. London, UK: Methuen, 1985.

"On *In a Different Voice:* An Interdisciplinary Forum." *Signs* 11, 2 (1986): 304-333.

Pajaczkowska, Claire. "Introduction to Kristeva." *m/f* 5-6 (1981): 149-157.

Psychanalyse et Politique. "Interview — 1974 [with Julia Kristeva]." Trans. Claire Pajaczkowska. *m/f* 5-6 (1981): 164-167.

Sandler, Joseph, et al., eds. *Freud's "On Narcissism: An Introduction"*. New Haven,CT: Yale University Press, 1991.

Smith, Joseph H. *Arguing with Lacan: Ego Psychology and Language*. New Haven,CT: Yale University Press, 1991.

"Special Symposium on Narcissism." *Telos* 44 (1980): 58-125.

"A Symposium: Christopher Lasch and the Culture of Narcissism." *Salmagundi* 46 (1979): 166-202.

Turkle, Sherry. *Psychoanalytic Politics: Freud's French Revolution*. Cambridge, MA: Massachusetts Institute of Technology University Press, 1981.

Woodward, Kathleen. "The Look and the Gaze: Narcissism, Aggression, and Aging." Working Paper No. 7. University of Wisconsin-Milwaukee: Center for Twentieth Century Studies, 1986.

FEMINIST CRITICISM

Christ, Carol P. *Diving Deep and Surfacing: Women Writers on Spiritual Quest*. Boston: Beacon Press, 1980.

de Lauretis, Teresa. "Semiotics and Experience." In *Alice Doesn't: Feminism, Semiotics, and Cinema*. Bloomington, IN: Indiana University Press, 1984.

DuPlessis, Rachel Blau. *Writing Beyond the Ending: Narrative Strategies of Twentieth-Century Women Writers*. Bloomington, IN: Indiana University Press, 1985.

French, Marilyn. *Beyond Power: On Women, Men, and Morals*. New York: Summit Books, 1985.

Greene, Gayle. *Changing the Story: Feminist Fiction and the Tradition*. Bloomington, IN: Indiana University Press, 1991.

Haraway, Donna. *Primate Visions: Gender, Race, and Nature in the World of Modern Science.* New York: Routledge, 1989.

Hirsch, Marianne. *The Mother/Daughter Plot: Narrative, Psychoanalysis, Feminism.* Bloomington, IN: Indiana University Press, 1989.

Janeway, Elizabeth. *Powers of the Weak.* New York: Morrow Quill, 1981.

Keyes, Claire. *The Aesthetics of Power: The Poetry of Adrienne Rich.* Athens, GA: University of Georgia Press, 1986.

LaBelle, Jenijoy. *Herself Beheld: The Literature of the Looking Glass.* Ithaca, NY: Cornell University Press, 1988.

Lips, Hilary M. *Women, Men, and Power.* Mountain View, CA: Mayfield Publishing Company, 1991.

Meese, Elizabeth A. *Crossing the Double-Cross: The Practice of Feminist Criticism.* Chapel Hill, NC: University of North Carolina Press, 1986.

Ostriker, Alicia Suskin. *Stealing the Language: The Emergence of Women's Poetry in America.* Boston: Beacon Press, 1986.

Rich, Adrienne. *Of Woman Born: Motherhood as Experience and Institution.* New York: W. W. Norton, 1976.

Rigney, Barbara Hill. *Madness and Sexual Politics in the Feminist Novel: Studies in Brontë, Woolf, Lessing, and Atwood.* Madison, WI: University of Wisconsin Press, 1978.

Rubenstein, Roberta. *Boundaries of the Self: Gender, Culture, Fiction.* Urbana, IL: University of Illinois Press, 1987.

Silverman, Kaja. *The Acoustic Mirror: The Female Voice in Psychoanalysis and Cinema.* Bloomington, IN: Indiana University Press, 1988.

Woolf, Virginia. *Three Guineas.* New York: Harcourt, Brace, and Co., 1938.

CRITICISM OF MARGARET ATWOOD'S WRITING

MONOGRAPHS

Davey, Frank. *Margaret Atwood: A Feminist Poetics.* Vancouver: Talonbooks, 1984.

Davidson, Arnold E., and Cathy N. Davidson, eds. *The Art of Margaret Atwood: Essays in Criticism.* Toronto: Anansi, 1981.

Grace, Sherrill E. *Violent Duality: A Study of Margaret Atwood.* Montreal: Véhicule Press, 1980.

———. and Lorraine Weir. eds. *Margaret Atwood: Language, Text, and System.* Vancouver: University of British Columbia Press, 1983.

McCombs, Judith, ed. *Critical Essays on Margaret Atwood.* Boston: G. K. Hall, 1988.

Mendez-Egle, Beatrice, ed. *Margaret Atwood: Reflection and Reality.* Edinburg, TX: Pan American University Press, 1987.

Rigney, Barbara Hill. *Margaret Atwood.* Totowa, NJ: Barnes and Noble, 1987.

Rosenberg, Jerome H. *Margaret Atwood.* Boston: Twayne, 1984.

VanSpanckeren, Kathryn, and Jan Garden Castro, eds. *Margaret Atwood: Vision and Forms.* Carbondale, IL: Southern Illinois University Press, 1988.

ON THE FICTION
Bodily Harm

Atherton, Stanley S. "Atwood, Horwood, Kreiner and Wright: The Caribbean Connection." In *Tensions between North and South: Studies in Modern Commonwealth Literature and Culture.* Ed. Edith Mettke, 28-36. Wurzburg: Konigshausen and Newmann, 1990.

Brydon, Diana. "Caribbean Revolution and Literary Convention." *Canadian Literature* 95 (1982): 181-185.

Hansen, Elaine Tuttle. "Fiction and (Post) Feminism in Atwood's *Bodily Harm.*" *Novel* 19, 1 (1985): 5-21.

Lynch, Denise E. "Personalist Plot in Atwood's *Bodily Harm.*" *Studies in the Humanities* 15, 1 (June 1988): 45-57.

Waelti-Walters, Jennifer. "Double-Read: On Margaret Atwood's *Bodily Harm*," *Room of One's Own* 8, 4 (1984): 116-122.

Wyatt, Jean. "Toward a More Creative Autonomy: *To the Lighthouse, Violet Clay, Bodily Harm*, 'How I Came to Write Fiction,' and *On Not Being Able to Paint*." In *Reconstructing Desire: The Role of the Unconscious in Women's Reading and Writing*. Chapel Hill, NC: University of North Carolina Press, 1990.

Cat's Eye

Banerjee, Chinmoy. "Atwood's Time: Hiding Art in *Cat's Eye*." *Modern Fiction Studies* 36, 4 (Winter 1990): 513-522.

Fulford, Robert. "Kernel of glass at the heart of new Atwood heroine." *Quill and Quire* (October 1988): 18.

Givner, Jessie. "Names, Faces and Signatures in Margaret Atwood's *Cat's Eye* and *The Handmaid's Tale*." *Canadian Literature* 133 (Summer 1992): 56-75.

Glover, Douglas. "Her life entire." *Books in Canada* (October 1988): 11-14.

James, Caryn. "Ambiguity Between Best Girlfriends." *The New York Times*, late edition, 28 January 1989, 16.

Kanfer, Stefan. "Time Arrested," *Time*, Canadian edition (6 February 1989): 66.

Lee, Hermione. "Little Women." *The New Republic* (10 April 1989): 38-40.

Lurie, Alison. "The Mean Years." *Ms.* (March 1989): 38, 41.

Mackay, Shena. "The painter's revenges." *Times Literary Supplement*, 3-9 February 1989, 113.

Manguel, Alberto. "First Impressions." *Saturday Night* (November 1988): 67-68, 70.

McCombs, Judith. "Contrary Re-memberings: The Creating Self and Feminism in *Cat's Eye*." *Canadian Literature* 129 (Summer 1991): 9-23.

McDermott, Alice. "What Little Girls Are Really Made Of." *The New York Times Book Review*, 5 February 1989, 1, 35.

"A Rich Talent for all Seasons." *Maclean's* (26 December 1989): 35.

Timson, Judith. "Atwood's Triumph." *Maclean's* (3 October 1988): 56-58.

Yglesias, Helen. "Odd Woman Out." *The Woman's Review of Books*, 6, 10-11 (July 1989): 3-4.

The Edible Woman

Brady, Elizabeth. "Towards a happier history: women and domination." In *Domination*. Ed. Alkis Kontos. Toronto: University of Toronto Press, 1975.

Keith, W. J. *Introducing Margaret Atwood's The Edible Woman: A Reader's Guide.* Toronto: ECW Press, 1989.

MacLulich, T. D. "Atwood's Adult Fairy Tale: Levi-Strauss, Bettelheim, and *The Edible Woman*." *Essays on Canadian Writing* 11 (1978): 111-129.

McMullen, Lorraine. "The Divided Self." *Atlantis* 5, 2 (1980): 52-67.

Patterson, Jayne. "The Taming of Externals: A Linguistic Study of Character Transformation in Margaret Atwood's *The Edible Woman*." *Studies in Canadian Literature* 7, 2 (1982): 151-167.

Rogers, Linda. "Margaret the Magician." *Canadian Literature* 60 (1974): 83-85.

Stow, Glenys. "Nonsense as Social Commentary in *The Edible Woman*." *Journal of Canadian Studies* 23, 3 (Fall 1988): 90-101.

Good Bones

Bemrose, John. "Moral miniatures: Margaret Atwood's latest work packs a punch." *Maclean's* (5 October 1992): 60-61.

Drobot, Eve. "Margaret Atwood, party girl." *The Globe and Mail*, 19 September 1992, C8.

Wigston, Nancy. "Atwood's Essence." *Quill and Quire* (October 1992): 21.

The Handmaid's Tale

Banerjee, Chinmoy. "Alice in Disneyland: Criticism as Commodity in *The Handmaid's Tale*." *Essays on Canadian Writing* 41 (Summer 1990): 74-92.

Bartkowski, Frances. "No Shadows without Light: Louky Bersianik's *The Eugelionne* and Margaret Atwood's *The Handmaid's Tale*." In *Feminist Utopias*. Lincoln, NB: University of Nebraska Press, 1989.

Bergmann, Harriet F. "'Teaching Them to Read': A Fishing Expedition in *The Handmaid's Tale*." *College English* 51, 8 (December 1989): 847-854.

Cowart, David. "The Way It Will Be: Puritanism and Patriarchy in *The Handmaid's Tale*." In *History and the Contemporary Novel.* Carbondale, IL: Southern Illinois University Press, 1989.

Davidson, Arnold E. "Future Tense: Making History in *The Handmaid's Tale*." In *Margaret Atwood: Vision and Forms.* Ed. Kathryn VanSpanckeren and Jan Garden Castro, Carbondale, IL: Southern Illinois University Press, 1988.

Deer, Glenn. "Rhetorical Strategies in *The Handmaid's Tale:* Dystopia and the Paradoxes of Power." *English Studies in Canada* 18, 2 (June 1992): 215-233.

Ferns, Chris. "The Value/s of Dystopia: *The Handmaid's Tale* and the Anti-Utopian Tradition." *Dalhousie Review* 69, 3 (Fall 1989): 73-382.

Fitting, Peter. "Recent Feminist Utopias: World Building and Strategies for Social Change." In *Mindscapes: The Geographies of Imagined Worlds.* Eds. George E. Slusser and Eric S. Rabkin, 155-163. Carbondale, IL: Southern Illinois University Press, 1989.

Garrett-Petts, W. F. "Reading, Writing, and the Postmodern Condition: Interpreting Margaret Atwood's *The Handmaid's Tale*." *Open Letter, 7th Series* 1 (Spring 1988): 74-92.

Greene, Gayle. "Choice of Evils," Review of *The Handmaid's Tale*, by Margaret Atwood. *The Women's Review of Books* 3, 10 (1986): 14-15.

Hammer, Stephanie Barbé. "The World As It Will Be? Female Satire and the Technology of Power in *The Handmaid's Tale*." *Modern Language Studies* 20, 2 (Spring 1990): 39-49.

Hjartarson, Paul. "The Literary Canon and Its Discontent: Reflections on the Cultural Reproduction of Value." In *Literatures in Canada.* Ed. Deborah C. Poff. *Canadian Issues* 10, 5 (1988): 67-80.

Kauffman, Linda. "Special Delivery: Twenty-first Century Epistolarity in *The Handmaid's Tale*." In *Writing the Female Voice: Essays on Epistolary Literature.* Ed. Elizabeth C. Goldsmith. Boston: Northeastern University Press, 1989.

Keith, W. J. "Apocalyptic Imaginations: Notes on Atwood's *The Handmaid's Tale* and Findley's *Not Wanted on the Voyage*." *Essays on Canadian Writing* 35 (Winter 1987): 123-134.

Ketterer, David. "Margaret Atwood's *The Handmaid's Tale:* A Contexutal Dystopia." *Science-Fiction Studies* 16, 2 (July 1989): 209-217.

Lacombe, Michele. "The Writing on the Wall: Amputated Speech in Margaret

Atwood's *The Handmaid's Tale.*" *Wascana Review* 21, 2 (Fall 1986): 3-20.

Larson, Janet L. "Margaret Atwood and the Future of Prophecy." *Religion and Literature* 21, 1 (Spring 1989): 27-61.

Malak, Amin. "Margaret Atwood's *The Handmaid's Tale* and the Dystopian Tradition." *Canadian Literature* 112 (1987): 9-16.

Miner, Madonne. "'Trust Me': Reading the Romance Plot in Margaret Atwood's *The Handmaid's Tale.*" *Twentieth Century Literature* 37, 2 (Summer 1991): 148-168.

Murphy, Patrick D. "Reducing the Dystopian Distance: Pseudo-Documentary Framing in Near-Future Fiction." *Science-Fiction Studies* 17 (1990): 25-40.

Nischik, Reingard M. "Back to the Future: Margaret Atwood's Anti-Utopian Vision in *The Handmaid's Tale.*" *Englisch-Amerikanische Studien* 5, 1 (1987): 139-148.

Norris, Ken. "'The University of Denay, Nunavit': The 'Historical Notes' in Margaret Atwood's *The Handmaid's Tale.*" *American Review of Canadian Studies* 20,3 (Autumn 1990): 357-364.

Rosenfelt, Deborah Silverton. "Feminism, 'Postfeminism,' and Contemporary Women's Fiction." In *Tradition and the Talents of Women.* Ed. Florence Howe, 268-291. Urbana, IL: Illinois University Press, 1991.

Rubenstein, Roberta. "Nature and Nurture in Dystopia: *The Handmaid's Tale.*" In *Margaret Atwood: Vision and Forms.* Eds. Kathryn VanSpanckeren and Jan Garden Castro, Carbondale, IL: Southern Illinois University Press, 1988.

Stimpson, Catharine R. "Atwood Woman." Review of *The Handmaid's Tale*, by Margaret Atwood. *The Nation* (31 May 1986): 764-767.

Widmer, Kingsley. "Antifemtopian Feminism and Atwood." In *Counterings: Utopian Dialectics in Contemporary Contexts.* Ann Arbor, MI: University of Michigan Research Press, 1988.

Lady Oracle

Beran, Carol L. "George, Leda, and a Poured Concrete Balcony: A Study of Three Aspects of the Evolution of *Lady Oracle.*" *Canadian Literature* 112 (1987): 18-28.

Freibert, Lucy M. "The Artist as Picaro: The Revelations of Margaret Atwood's *Lady Oracle.*" *Canadian Literature* 92 (1982): 23-33.

Givner, Jessie. "Mirror Images in Margaret Atwood's *Lady Oracle.*" *Studies in Canadian Literature* 14, 1 (1989): 139-146.

Godard, Barbara. "My (m)Other, My Self: Strategies for Subversion in Atwood and Hébert." *Essays on Canadian Writing* 26 (1983): 13-44.

Hite, Molly. "Other Side, Other Woman." In her *The Other Side of the Story,* 127-167. Ithaca, NY: Cornell University Press, 1989.

———."Writing — and Re-writing — the Body: Female Sexuality and Feminist Fiction." *Feminist Studies* 14, 1 (Spring 1988): 121-142.

Jensen, Emily. "Margaret Atwood's *Lady Oracle:* A Modern Parable." *Essays on Canadian Writing* 33 (1986): 29-49.

Rao, Eleonora. "Margaret Atwood's *Lady Oracle:* Writing Against Notions of Unity." *British Journal of Canadian Studies* 4, 1 (1989): 136-156.

Rosowski, Susan J. "Margaret Atwood's *Lady Oracle:* Social Mythology and the Gothic Novel." *Research Studies* 49, 2 (1981): 87-98.

Ross, Catherine Sheldrick. "'Banished To This Other Place': Atwood's *Lady Oracle.*" *English Studies in Canada* 6, 4 (1980): 460-474.

Rule, Jane. "Life, Liberty and the Pursuit of Normalcy: The Novels of Margaret Atwood." *The Malahat Review* 41 (January 1977): 42-49.

Sciff-Zamaro, Roberta. "The Re/membering of the Female Power in *Lady Oracle.*" *Canadian Literature* 112 (1987): 32-38.

Vincent, Sybil Korff. "The Mirror and the Cameo: Margaret Atwood's Comic/Gothic Novel, *Lady Oracle.*" In *The Female Gothic.* Ed. Juliann E. Fleenor. Montreal: Eden Press, 1983.

Life Before Man

Beran, Carol L. "The Canadian Mosaic: Functional Ethnicity in Margaret Atwood's *Life Before Man.*" *Essays on Canadian Writing* 41 (Summer 1990): 59-73.

Carrington, Ildiko de Papp. "Demons, Doubles, and Dinosaurs: *Life Before Man, The Origin of Consciousness,* and 'The Icicle.'" *Essays on Canadian Writing* 33 (1986): 68-88.

Goetsch, Paul. "Margaret Atwood's *Life Before Man* as a Novel of Manners." In *Gaining Ground: European Critics on Canadian Literature.* Eds. Robert Kroetsch and Reingard M. Nischik. Edmonton: NeWest, 1985, 1988.

Surfacing

Allen, Carolyn. "Failures of Word, Uses of Silence: Djuna Barnes, Adrienne Rich, and Margaret Atwood." *Regionalism and the Female Imagination* 4, 1 (1978): 1-7.

Bartlett, Donald R. "'Fact' and Form in *Surfacing*." *The University of Windsor Review* 17, 1 (1982): 21-28.

Beckman, Susan, "Language as Cultural Identity in Achebe, Ihimaera, Laurence, and Atwood." *World Literature Written in English* 20, 1 (1981): 117-134.

Berryman, Charles. "Atwood's Narrative Quest." *The Journal of Narrative Technique* 17, 1 (1987): 51-56.

Bjerring, Nancy E. "The Problem of Language in Margaret Atwood's *Surfacing*." *Queen's Quarterly* 83, 4 (1976): 597-612.

Bowering, George. "Desire and the Unnamed Narrator." *Descant* 19, 3 (Fall 1988): 18-24.

Cederstrom, Lorelei. "The Regeneration of Time in Atwood's *Surfacing*." *Atlantis* 6, 2 (1981): 24-37.

Clark, Meera T. "Margaret Atwood's *Surfacing*: Language, Logic and the Art of Fiction." *Modern Poetry Studies* 13, 3 (1983): 2-15.

Donaldson, Mara E. "Woman as Hero in Margaret Atwood's *Surfacing* and Maxine Hong Kingston's *The Woman Warrior*." In *Heroines of Popular Culture*. Ed. Ray Browne. Bowling Green, OH: Bowling Green State University Popular Press, 1987.

Gerson, Carole. "Margaret Atwood and Quebec: A Footnote on *Surfacing*." *Studies in Canadian Literature* 1,1 (1976): 115-119.

Gerstenberger, Donna. "Conceptions Literary and Otherwise: Women Writers and the Modern Imagination." *Novel* 9, 2 (1976): 141-150.

Gray, Francine du Plessix. "Margaret Atwood: Nature as the Nunnery." In *Adam and Eve and the City: Selected Nonfiction*. New York: Simon & Schuster, 1987.

Hinz, Evelyn J. "The Masculine/Feminine Psychology of American/Canadian Primitivism: *Deliverance* and *Surfacing*." In *Other Voices, Other Views: An International Collection of Essays from the Bicentennial*. Ed. Robin W. Winks. Westport, CT: Greenwood Press, 1978.

————. "The Religious Roots of the Feminine Identity Issue: Margaret Laurence's *The Stone Angel* and Margaret Atwood's *Surfacing*." In *Margaret Laurence: An Appreciation*. Ed. Christl Verduyn. Peterborough, ON: Broadview Press, 1988.

————, and John J. Teunissen. "*Surfacing*: Margaret Atwood's 'Nymph Complaining.'" *Contemporary Literature* 29, 2 (1979): 221-236.

Homans, Margaret. "'Her Very Own Howl': The Ambiguities of Representation in Recent Women's Fiction." *Signs* 9, 2 (1983): 186-205.

James, William C. "Atwood's *Surfacing*." *Canadian Literature* 91 (1981): 174-181.

Jones, Anne G. "Margaret Atwood." *The Hollins Critic* 16, 3 (June 1979): 12.

Klovan, Peter. "'They Are Out of Reach Now': The Family Motif in Margaret Atwood's *Surfacing*." *Essays on Canadian Writing* 33 (1986): 1-28.

Kokotailo, Philip. "Form in Atwood's *Surfacing*." *Studies in Canadian Literature* 8, 2 (1983): 155-165.

Mackenzie, Manfred. "'I am a place': *Surfacing* and Spirit of Place." In *A Sense of Place in the New Literatures in English*. Ed. Peggy Nightingale. St. Lucia: University of Queensland Press, 1986.

Murray, Heather. "The Synthetic Habit of Mind: Margaret Atwood's *Surfacing*." *World Literature Written in English* 25, 1 (1985): 89-104.

Quigley, Theresia. "*Surfacing*: A Critical Study." *The Antigonish Review* 34 (1978): 77-87.

Robertson, Esther. "The Politics of Relationships." M.A. Thesis. University of British Columbia, 1974.

Robinson, Sally. "The 'Anti-Logos Weapon': Multiplicity in Women's Texts." *Contemporary Literature* 29, 1 (Spring 1988): 105-124.

Ross, Catherine Sheldrick. "A Singing Spirit: Female Rites of Passage in *Klee Wyck*, *Surfacing*, and *The Diviners*" *Atlantis* 4, 1 (Fall 1978): 86-94.

Rubenstein, Roberta. "*Surfacing*: Margaret Atwood's Journey to the Interior." *Modern Fiction Studies* 22, 3 (1976): 387-399.

Schaeffer, Susan Fromberg. "'It Is Time that Separates Us': Margaret Atwood's *Surfacing*." *The Centennial Review* 18, 4 (1974): 319-337.

Sullivan, Rosemary. "Breaking the Circle." *The Malahat Review* 41 (January 1977): 30-41.

———. "*Surfacing* and *Deliverance*." *Canadian Literature* 67 (1976): 6-20.

Sweetapple, Rosemary. "Margaret Atwood: Victims and Survivors." *Southern Review* [Adelaide] 9, 1 (1976): 50-69.

Thomas, Sue. "Mythic Reconception and the Mother/Daughter Relationship in Margaret Atwood's *Surfacing*." *Ariel* 19, 2 (April 1988): 73-85.

Wilderness Tips

Bemrose, John. "Studies in suffering." *Maclean's* (16 September 1991): 58.

Fawcett, Brian. "Scouting the Future." *Books in Canada* (October 1991): 29-32.

Hussein, Aamer. "Strategies for survival." *Times Literary Supplement*, 13 September 1991, 20.

Jones, Daniel. "Atwood's Dark Parables, Davies's Ballad of Bankruptcy." *Quill and Quire* (August 1991): 14.

Wilcox, James. "The Hairball on the Mantelpiece." *The New York Times Book Review*, 24 November 1991, 7.

GENERAL STUDIES OF THE FICTION

Buss, Helen. "Maternality and Narrative Strategies in the Novels of Margaret Atwood." *Atlantis* 15, 1 (Fall 1989): 76-83.

Keith, W. J. "Margaret Atwood." In *A Sense of Style: Studies in the Art of Fiction in English-Speaking Canada*. Toronto: ECW Press, 1989.

Langer, Beryl Donaldson. "Class and Gender in Margaret Atwood's Fiction." *Australian-Canadian Studies* 6, 1 (1988): 73-101.

Parsons, Ann. "The Self-Inventing Self: Women Who Lie and Pose in the Fiction of Margaret Atwood." In *Gender Studies: New Directions in Feminist Criticism*. Ed. Judith Spector. Bowling Green, OH: Bowling Green State University Popular Press, 1986.

ON THE POETRY
The Animals in that Country

Ross, Gary. "The Divided Self." *Canadian Literature* 71 (1976):39-47.

The Circle Game

Ross, Gary. "The Circle Game." *Canadian Literature* 60 (1974):51-63.

The Journals of Susanna Moodie

Bilan, R. P. "Margaret Atwood's *The Journals of Susanna Moodie*." *Canadian Poetry* 2 (1978): 1-12.

Davidson, Arnold E. "The Different Voices in Margaret Atwood's *The Journals of Susanna Moodie*," *The CEA Critic* 43, 1 (1980): 14-20.

Glicksohn, Susan Wood. "The Martian Point of View." *Extrapolation* 15, 2 (1974): 161-173.

Groening, Laura. "*The Journals of Susanna Moodie*: A Twentieth-Century Look at a Nineteenth-Century Life." *Canadian Literature* 8, 2 (1983): 166-180.

Lane, Patrick. "The Unyielding Phrase." *Canadian Literature* 122-123 (Autumn-Winter 1989): 57-64.

Power Politics

Waters, Katherine E. "Margaret Atwood." In MOTHER *was not a person*. Ed. Margret Andersen. Montreal: Black Rose Books, 1972.

True Stories

Weiner, Deborah. "'Difference That Kills'/Difference That Heals: Representing Latin America in the Poetry of Elizabeth Bishop and Margaret Atwood." In *Comparative Literature East and West: Traditions and Trends*. Eds. Cornelia Moore and Raymond A. Moody. Honolulu, HI: College of Languages, Linguistics, and Literature, University of Hawaii and the East-West Center, 1989.

Two-Headed Poems

Henneberger, Sandra. "Strange and Playful Paradigms in Margaret Atwood's Poetry." *Women's Studies* 17 (1990): 277-288.

McCombs, Judith. "Atwood's fictive portraits of the artist: from victim to surfacer, from oracle to birth." *Women's Studies* 12; (1986): 69-88.

You Are Happy

Dilliott, Maureen. "Emerging from the Cold: Margaret Atwood's *You Are Happy*." *Modern Poetry Studies* 8, 1 (1977): 73-90.

Johnston, Gordon. "'The Ruthless Story and the Future Tense' in Margaret Atwood's 'Circe/Mud Poems.'" *Canadian Literature* (1980): 167-176.

GENERAL STUDIES OF THE POETRY

Davey, Frank. "Atwood's Gorgon Touch." *Studies in Canadian Literature* 2, 2 (1977): 146-163.

Foster, John Wilson. "The Poetry of Margaret Atwood." *Canadian Literature* 74 (1977): 5-20.

Godard, Barbara. "Telling It Over Again: Atwood's Art of Parody." *Canadian Poetry* 21 (Fall-Winter 1987): 1-30.

Irvine, Lorna. "The Red and Silver Heroes Have Collapsed." *Concerning Poetry* 12, 2 (1979): 59-68.

Jones, D. G. "Cold Eye and Optic Heart: Marshall McLuhan and Some Canadian Poets." *Modern Poetry Studies* 5, 2 (1974): 170-187.

Lilienfeld, Jane. "Silence and Scorn in a Lyric of Intimacy: The Progress of Margaret Atwood's Poetry." *Women's Studies* 7, 1/2 (1980): 185-194.

TREATMENTS OF MIRROR IMAGERY IN THE FICTION OR POETRY

Ewell, Barbara C, "The Language of Alienation in Margaret Atwood's *Surfacing*." *The Centennial Review* 25 (1981): 185-202.

Maclean, Susan. "*Lady Oracle:* The Art of Reality and the Reality of Art." *Journal of Canadian Fiction* 28/29 (1980): 179-197.

TREATMENTS OF NARCISSISM

Wilson, Sharon R. "The Fragmented Self in *Lady Oracle*." *Commonwealth Novel in English* 1 (1982): 50-85.

GENERAL STUDIES OF ATWOOD'S WRITING

Bowering, George. "Margaret Atwood's Hands." *Studies in Canadian Literature* 6,1 (1981): 39-52.

Brown, Russell M. "Atwood's Sacred Wells." *Essays on Canadian Writing* 17 (1980): 5-43.

Davey, Frank. "Atwood Walking Backwards." *Open Letter.* Second series, 5 (1973): 74-84.

Griffith, Margaret. "Verbal Terrain in the Novels of Margaret Atwood." *Critique* 21, 3 (1980), 85-93.

Hutcheon, Linda. "Process, Product, and Politics: The Postmodernism of Margaret Atwood." In *The Canadian Postmodern: A Study of Contemporary English-Canadian Fiction.* Toronto: Oxford University Press, 1988.

————. "'Shape Shifters': Canadian Women Writers and the Tradition." In *The Canadian Postmodern: A Study of Contemporary English-Canadian Fiction.* Toronto: Oxford University Press, 1988.

Jones, Anne G. "Margaret Atwood: Songs of the Transformer, Songs of the Transformed." *The Hollins Critic* 16, 3 (1979): 1-15.

Mansbridge, Francis, "Search for Self in the Novels of Margaret Atwood." *Journal of Canadian Fiction* 22 (1978): 106-117.

McDonald, Larry. "Psychologism and the Philosophy of Progress: The Recent Fiction of MacLennan, Davies, and Atwood." *Studies in Canadian Literature* 9,2 (1984): 121-143.

Onley, Gloria. "Power Politics in Bluebeard's Castle." *Canadian Literature* 60 (1974): 21-42.

Piercy, Marge. "Margaret Atwood: Beyond Victimhood." *The American Poetry Review* 2, 6 (1973): 41-44.

Robertson, Esther. "The Politics of Relationships." M.A. Thesis. University of British Columbia, 1974.

Sandler, Linda, ed. "Margaret Atwood: A Symposium." *The Malahat Review* 41 (1977).

Stovel, Nora Foster. "Reflections on Mirror Images: Doubles and Identity in the Novels of Margaret Atwood." *Essays on Canadian Writing* 33 (1986): 50-67.

❖

PERMISSIONS

All the following titles are by Margaret Atwood.
Publishers' permissions are listed by country.

OTHER BOOKS FROM SECOND STORY PRESS